DATE DUE

The Psychology of Parental Control

How Well-Meant Parenting Backfires

Wendy S. Grolnick
Clark University

LAWRENCE ERLBAUM ASSOCIATES, PUBLISHERS

2003   Mahwah, New Jersey   London

Lawrence Erlbaum Associates, Inc., Publishers
10 Industrial Avenue
Mahwah, NJ 07430

Cover design by Kathryn Houghtaling Lacey

Library of Congress Cataloging-in-Publication Data

Grolnick, Wendy S.
The psychology of parental control : how well-meant parenting backfires /
    Wendy S. Grolnick.
          p. cm.
        Includes bibliographical references and index.
    ISBN 0-8058-3540-7 (cloth : alk. paper)
    ISBN 0-8058-3541-5 (pbk. : alk. paper)
    1. Parent and child—Psychological aspects. 2. Parenting—Psychological
      aspects. 3. Control (Psychology). 4. Parents—Psychology. I. Title.
    HQ755.85 G74   2002
    306.874 —dc21   2001051087
                                                              CIP

Books published by Lawrence Erlbaum Associates are printed on acid-free
paper, and their bindings are chosen for strength and durability.

Printed in the United States of America
10 9 8 7 6 5 4 3 2

Contents

Acknowledgments

Many individuals contributed to this book, either directly or indirectly. I'd like to start by acknowledging the two individuals who introduced me to self-determination theory: Richard Ryan and Edward Deci. As a graduate student at the University of Rochester, I became fascinated by this theory and the work of these two brilliant and creative individuals. It was through their eyes that I saw the important ramifications of this theory for child development and for parenting. I am grateful for the opportunity to have studied under these wonderful mentors.

I also acknowledge the many students who collaborated on the studies described in this book—among them Suzanne Gurland, Carolyn Kurowski, Wendy DeCourcey, Karen Jacob, Corina Benjet, Margaret Sewell, Kristine Landry, Laurie Weiss, and Melanie Farkas. The design of many of the studies described reflects their contribution, the completion of the studies their hard work and commitment. The support of Clark University and my Clark colleagues, particularly Michael Addis and Jamie McHale, is also gratefully acknowledged.

I owe a great deal to all of the parents and children who took the time to participate in my studies. Without their openness and willingness to share their lives, the work could not have occurred. A number of principals allowed us access to their families and supported my work. Among them, Matthew Ryan, Anthony Caputo, and Judy Finkel were particularly helpful.

The completion of a book is always harder than anticipated. I began the book on my sabbatical during the 1998–1999 academic year. I had hoped to finish it by the end of the year. Two years later I was still plugging along. I could not have maintained my enthusiasm without the help of supportive family and friends. On one particularly stressful day, when I was stuck in the midst of a chapter, I contemplated putting the project on hold. Then I heard my daughter Allison talking to a friend on the phone, proudly informing her that "my mom is writing a book." Back to the chapter I went. My two daughters, Allison and Rebecca, have been a source of many of the parenting stories woven into the book and to my thinking about parental control more generally. I am grateful to them for their love and the tolerance they've had for my parenting mistakes. My father, Simon Grolnick, was a source of inspiration for me—his love of a good idea and intellectual spirit was contagious. I proudly watched him write several wonderful books. I hope that he would have liked this one.

Several friends and family members were kind enough to share their parenting experiences and to provide support to me through the writing process. Maxine Grolnick, Judy Tullie, Elizabeth Mirro, Debbie Godwin, Candy Weiner, Maria Markenson, Lori Saffer, Susan Merrell, Laurie Skole, Janine Idelson, and Diane Rosenkrantz listened to and responded to many of my ideas.

I am indebted to Lou Ann Walker, a wonderful writer who worked with me on the form and wording of the book. Not only did she bring life to some of the more stodgy academic writing, but she also shared her own insights and experiences with me. Lou Ann was particularly creative with the anecdotes at the beginning of each chapter.

I extend many thanks to the individuals at Lawrence Erlbaum Associates who facilitated the publishing of this book. While she was at Erlbaum, Judi Amsel read the proposal and supported the project from the start. Her enthusiasm and advice were crucial in the early stages of the book. Bill Webber and Erica Kica were invariably helpful and moved the process smoothly to completion.

I greatly acknowledge the financial generosity of several organizations without whose support this work would not be possible: the William T. Grant Foundation, the Spencer Foundation, and the National Institute of Mental Health. The William T. Grant Foundation Faculty Scholar award allowed me to connect with many talented scholars whose ideas influenced my work.

Finally, I owe my biggest debt of gratitude to my husband, Jay: he believed in my ability to write this book from the start and gave me encouragement and time when I needed it. His endless love and support allow me to be the researcher and parent I am.

Introduction

When Courtney brought her home report card with three Cs—two more than in the previous grading period—her parents were upset. Feeling they had to act quickly to be sure Courtney did better the next time, they came up with a "positive approach." Signing the report card the following morning, her mother made an announcement: "For every A you bring home next grading period, I'll give you $10," she told Courtney. "For every B, $5."

Lily's parents were shocked and dismayed when her report card turned up with all those Cs. They told her how disappointed they were. "We were very displeased last grading period. You let us down again." For the next few days, the atmosphere in Lily's house was noticeably chilly. Her parents spoke only to answer questions. Their plan was to get to Lily. By behaving this way, they were trying to convey just how distressed they were.

What do these approaches have in common? In each scenario the parents are concerned and involved. They are taking action in order to change the situation. But which of these responses is controlling? The first one, a positive approach that uses rewards, or the second one, which employs a negative approach, using criticism in order to evoke guilt? According to many people, the latter example would clearly fall into the "controlling" category, for there is some, although not complete, consensus that critical, hostile behavior with the threat of withdrawal of love is controlling (e.g., B. K. Barber, 1996).

Consider, however, Courtney's parents' solution to the dilemma of the lackluster report card. They decided to use positive reinforcement. Praise, rewards, and positive reinforcement are often considered conducive to children's development.

Herein lies the central issue. I would argue that the responses of both Courtney's and Lily's parents are controlling. Each girl experiences a similar pressure as a result of her parents' behavior. Each girl feels a pressure to perform. The bottom line is that both approaches have a similar goal: to coerce the child into changing her behavior. Both sets of parents have their eyes focused on the outcome: grades. In Courtney's case, the pressure comes from the promise of a desired reward. In the other case, the pressure comes because Lily fears the loss of her parents' love and their positive regard, as well as their anger and disappointment. Both sets of parents proceed as if they have the answer to their child's problem.

If either of these children pursues her studies more intensely, she will be doing so for a purpose that is separate from her own desires. In one case it will be to obtain money, in the other to avoid parental wrath. In neither case will the child have a sense of agency, a sense of being the one to initiate changes in her own behavior. She will not have a sense that her behavior emanates from her or that she is an agent in her own life. In neither case will the behavior stem from her *own* beliefs that the pursuit of good grades is important and meaningful in and of itself.

Just what is parental control? The concept is not new. Indeed, it has been a focus in much of the research on parenting during the last 50 years. Within the research community the topic of parental control has been addressed with a variety of terms, each with its own meaning. They include psychological control versus psychological autonomy (B. K. Barber, 1996; Schaefer, 1959, 1965a); democratic versus autocratic parenting (Baldwin, 1948); authoritarian versus authoritative styles (Baumrind, 1965, 1967; Steinberg, Elmen, & Mounts, 1989); power-assertive and non-power-assertive techniques (Hoffman, 1970); and, in my own work based on self-determination theory (Deci & Ryan, 1985b), controlling versus autonomy-supportive parenting (Grolnick & Ryan, 1989; Grolnick, Ryan, & Deci, 1997). Control has been viewed as a type of technique, a style of using techniques, and a more psychological concept without reference to how it is communicated to children (Darling & Steinberg, 1993). The term *control* has been used by various researchers to refer to different phenomena; some use it to refer to demands for maturity (Baumrind, 1965) or efforts to manage children's lives (Barber, 1996), and others use it to refer to the way demands are communicated (Grolnick & Ryan, 1989). Such different uses of the same term have led to controversies about whether control is beneficial or detrimental to children and to much confusion about the concept itself.

Part of this confusion stems from the fact that many definitions confuse the notions of being *controlling* and being *in control*. When parents—and even some professionals—hear that I am advocating lower levels of controlling behaviors, they balk. They think that I am suggesting that parents should give up their roles as authorities in their children's lives and relinquish their responsibilities to provide discipline and standards of conduct for their children.

This could not be further from the truth. In this book I clearly delineate the positive effects of being in control from the negative ones of being controlling.

Can professionals and parents possibly come to a consensus about the meaning of being controlling? I believe they can. Although the various terms researchers use to refer to controlling parenting differ in many ways, they all suggest parenting that involves pushes or pressures for children to think, feel, or behave in specific ways. When parents communicate in controlling ways, they undermine their children's ability to initiate their own actions and instead induce children to behave because of external or internal pressures (Grolnick, Deci, & Ryan, 1997). Parental communication that is controlling is likely to lead to compliance in which the child outwardly conforms to the parents' directives, or it can lead to reactance, wherein the directives are defied, either subtly or overtly. The result is that the communication is not effective in bringing about the positive changes in the child that parents wish to make. Furthermore, it may have detrimental side effects for the parent-child relationship.

As we will see, parental control does not simply mean yelling or using physical punishment. Neither is it the result of parents having bad—or good—intentions. Some parents' most controlling behavior comes from their desire to provide the very best for their children and to be certain that their children are not missing out on a single opportunity. Mothers and fathers need to assure themselves that they aren't wasting their children's talents or skills. Neither is control a question of using either negative or positive approaches. Parents and other caretakers can control through physical punishment, but they can also control through rewards and even praise.

If parental control is one end of the continuum, what is its opposite? One answer is parents' support of autonomy in their children. Autonomy support is an active process, which involves taking a child's frame of reference, supporting independent problem solving, and involving the child in creating rules and structures. Using this approach, parents also provide choices for children and encourage their children to initiate their own activities. The goal of autonomy-supportive parenting is to facilitate a sense of self-initiation in children and to support their active attempts to solve their own problems.

Let's go back to the report card example. Sam brought home a less-than-glowing report card. The family's response was to sit down as a group and find out Sam's perception of what had gone awry that grading period. The next step was to consider steps Sam could take: Should the family establish an inviolable homework time? Should Sam get tutoring from his teacher? The family may even need to set up consequences if Sam's grades don't improve; for example, Sam might need to withdraw from one of his extracurricular activities. The point, however, is that the family engaged in a dialogue that included Sam, and then Sam was involved in the decision-making process. In the last part of this book I examine autonomy support and explore how parents can implement autonomy-supportive parenting in the realms of school, sports, and social activities.

Given both interest in the concept of control and confusion in the research literature, the subject of controlling parental behavior is extremely timely. On television and in newspapers and magazines we are bombarded with examples that range from the almost laughable to the egregious. A recent *New York Times* article (New York Times, July 16, 2000) talked about ways in which parents subtly tried to choose their children's elementary school teachers. There have been many stories condemning parents who put their children into beauty pageants for their own gain. Screaming parents on the sidelines of softball and soccer games have become almost a cliche. Yet even that example can have horrifying ramifications: Recently one father killed another at their children's hockey game in Massachusetts because of a rivalry on the ice.

I begin this book by examining the concept of control, and I describe what research has taught us about the effects of control on children's development. Then I discuss specific ways that parents control—from the overt and obvious methods, which include physical punishment, to the more covert methods, such as controlling praise. I then examine the effects of control on various goals that parents may have for their kids, ranging from the short-term goal of assuring their children's compliance to the long-term goal of fostering the child's internalizing, or taking responsibility for, the regulation of his or her own behavior. The effects of control on these goals can be drastically different.

One of my major aims is to provide an understanding of factors that lead parents to control. These include environmental and economic stresses and strains as well as characteristics of the child that "pull" for more or less control. Beyond this, I emphasize another sort of pull or pressure: that from within the parent. Even parents who value autonomy may find their own self-esteem becoming "hooked" to their children's achievements, a process called *ego involvement* (Sherif & Cantril, 1947). When parents become ego involved in their child's performance, the result is likely to be increased control. In illustrating this phenomenon I draw on studies in the motivation literature that have focused on teachers and college students (e.g., Deci, Spiegel, Ryan, Koestner, & Kauffman, 1982) as well as on my own studies of parents. I also include work on *parental investment*, which has explored the biological, environmental, and historical origins of parents' psychological investment in their children and how that investment leads parents to focus on products rather than process in their children.

The work I share here on parental control is the culmination of what I have learned in studying the development of autonomy as a researcher and clinician for 18 years and as a mother for 10. This book stems, in part, from my own experience struggling in a competitive world to keep the faith that the autonomy support I attempt to provide my children will ultimately serve them well.

The things I have learned include the following.

1. Parental control can be subtle; it lurks in many of the approaches parenting experts advocate.
2. Parental control undermines the very behaviors we wish to inculcate in our children.
3. Supporting children's autonomy is a challenge, even when parents are committed to doing so.

This book is intended to provide an understanding of parental control, its meaning, its determinants, and its consequences. I have oriented the work to a variety of readers, including scholars, clinicians, students, and parents alike. To speak to such a broad readership, I have adopted a style that combines research and theory with my own and others' experiences, as well as examples from everyday life. I hope that this approach will give the reader a knowledge base as well as experiential feel for the issue of parental control in everyday life. After all, each one of us plays multiple roles in our lives. We are, at once, students, purveyors, and recipients of control.

1

The Concept of Control

Not so very long ago, Ellen Perkins took her 7-year-old daughter, Hannah, dress shopping for a special occasion. They started out at a store near their house. Hannah looked adorable in the pink chiffon she tried on, but Hannah hated pink. Her mother was exasperated but agreed to go to the mall to look some more. The problem was that Mrs. Perkins was already strapped for time. The mall was 30 minutes away. When they arrived at the mall, Mrs. Perkins decided to try to check one more thing off her list. Hannah's bangs were in her eyes. "Let's get those bangs trimmed right here," Mrs. Perkins said.

Hannah refused. "No! I don't trust those haircutters!"

Mrs. Perkins, already stressed, reacted: "If you don't get your hair cut, then we'll go home right now. You won't get a dress."

"Fine," Hannah said.

Not getting what she wanted, Mrs. Perkins decided to up the ante of control. "If you don't get your bangs cut, then I'm not going to get the present you want to get for your friend, and no one else will buy it either."

Hannah started to cry.

In this case, the increasing pressure and force applied by Mrs. Perkins signals control, but just what does it mean to be controlling? In this chapter I explore the concept of control. I discuss terms such as *psychological control, autocratic parenting,* and *the authoritarian style,* and I contrast those styles with *psychological autonomy, democratic parenting,* and *the authoritative style.* On the basis of this work, I differentiate the concept of being "in control" from that of being "controlling." I will also contrast the ideas of involvement and control. One question I explore later is: When does involvement become controlling?

PARENTING DIMENSIONS

The literature on parenting is replete with a sometimes-confusing array of terms to describe parenting types and dimensions. Researchers have used terms such as *responsive parenting, sensitive parenting, democratic versus autocratic*, and *restrictive versus nonrestrictive*. Trying to determine what makes for "good" parenting means wading through these terms—and more. Often the meaning is unclear from the label and readers have to judge a particular researcher's usage and intent and evaluate the way in which parenting dimensions are measured. The task is complicated even more by the fact that the same term can have different meanings to different researchers.

The terminology mire can be daunting. It can appear that no two researchers are studying the same concepts, much less yielding consistent findings. However, when parenting questionnaires, made up of multiple self-report parenting items, or ratings of parents drawn from observations, have been factor analyzed during the last 35 years, two dimensions consistently emerge. Regardless of what they are called, they appear to be reliably tapping two key parenting dimensions.

The first dimension has been variously called *parental warmth, acceptance, responsivity*, and *child-centeredness*. Figure 1.1 presents a list of some of these terms. In general the dimension refers to parents providing emotional and material resources to their children. In my own work I have referred to this dimension as *involvement*.

Earl Schaefer (1959) suggested that parents could be placed along a warmth–hostility dimension, with ratings of high affection, positive reinforcement, and sensitivity to the child's needs and desires at one end and rejection and hostility at the other. Alfred Baldwin (1955) and Wesley Becker (1964) found evidence of a dimension that ranged from warmth to coolness. Lea Pulkkinen (1982) distinguished parent-centered versus child-centered parenting, and G. Parker, Tupling, and Brown (1979), using the Parent Bonding Instrument, identified caring and empathic parenting versus rejecting or indifferent parenting. Diana Baumrind's (1967) typological scheme identifies authoritative parents as warm and accepting and authoritarian parents as cool and aloof. Researchers who hold an attachment perspective posit that children develop secure attachments to their caregivers through available, responsive parenting (Sroufe & Waters, 1977).

Evidence for the underlying correspondence of these differently named constructs comes from the fact that each construct predicts similar qualities in chil-

PARENTING DIMENSION 1

- **Warmth vs. Hostility** (Schaefer, 1959)
- **Warmth vs. Coolness** (Becker, 1964)
- **Child-Centeredness** (Pulkkinen, 1982)
- **Caring and Empathic vs. Rejecting and Indifferent**
  (G. Parker et al., 1979)
- **Involvement** (Grolnick & Slowiaczek, 1994)
- **Acceptance vs. Rejection** (Rohner, 1986)

FIG. 1.1.   Parenting Dimension 1.

dren. Warmth was found to be associated with children's higher self-esteem in classic studies by Coopersmith (1967). Parental involvement has been linked to children's self-esteem (Loeb, Horst, & Horton, 1980) as well as to higher levels of achievement and motivation and lower levels of delinquency and aggression (Hatfield, Ferguson, & Alpert, 1967). I present these facts without elaboration for now, but later I argue that the effects of warmth and involvement depend on other dimensions. Nonetheless, at this point we can conclude that warm, responsive, and involved caretaking yields positive effects.

The second dimension that emerges in the majority of parenting studies is far more perplexing than involvement. What unites this second dimension as it emerges across various studies is its relation to control. Descriptions of this dimension include *controlling versus permissive, firm control versus lax control, psychological control versus psychological autonomy, restrictive versus permissive,* and *controlling versus autonomy supportive* (see Fig. 1.2 for a list of some of these terms). How have different researchers understood this dimension?

EARLY CONCEPTS OF CONTROL

Baldwin's (1948) groundbreaking investigation of child rearing conducted at the Fels Research Institute in the 1940s was one of the first to examine systematically the idea of parental control. Baldwin interviewed the parents of 67 children, beginning when the children were 4 years old then observing the parents and children every 6 months afterward. On the basis of the interviews and observations he rated children and parents on a number of dimensions, including sensitivity, impatience, and affectionateness. Factor analysis of the ratings of parents yielded two general factors: Control and Democracy. Control, as defined by Baldwin, "emphasizes the existence of restrictions upon behavior which are clearly con-

PARENTING DIMENSION 2

- **Democratic vs. Autocratic** (Baldwin, 1948)
- **Firm Control vs. Lax Control** (Baumrind, 1965)
- **Psychological Control vs. Psychological Autonomy**
  (Schaefer, 1959)
- **Controlling vs. Autonomy Supportive**
  (Deci & Ryan, 1985b)
- **Restrictive vs. Permissive** (Becker, 1964)

FIG. 1.2.   Parenting Dimension 2.

veyed to the child" (p. 130). Democracy involved high levels of verbal contact between parent and child and openness of communication. In democratic parenting, polices are arrived at by mutual agreement, reasons are given for disciplinary actions, and the child's input in parenting decisions is sought when possible. Control and Democracy were positively correlated.

Thus in Baldwin's (1948) study, control refers to the limits, rules, and restrictions placed on children's behavior. For Baldwin, control was positive. However, although control and democracy tended to be correlated, it was possible to have control within the context of democratic or more autocratic parenting.

What effects do these parenting characteristics have on children? Keeping control constant, Baldwin (1948) found that democracy produces an aggressive, fearless, and playful child who tends to be a leader but also who is cruel to his or her peers. With democracy held constant, control decreases quarrelsomeness, negativism, and disobedience. Occurring together, control and lack of democracy create a quiet, well-behaved child who is low in creativity. The best outcomes were observed in homes in which there was a great deal of interaction between parents and children, along with democracy.

Becker (1964) proposed two factors of parenting: restrictiveness versus permissiveness and warmth versus hostility. He characterized the restrictive end as having "restrictions and strict enforcement of demands in the areas of sex play, modesty behavior, table manners, toilet training, neatness, orderliness, care of household furniture, noise, obedience, aggression to siblings, aggression to peers, and aggression to parents" (p. 174). The permissive end included fewer restrictions, and the enforcement was less firm. Becker crossed the two dimensions to yield four types of parents: warm–restrictive, warm–permissive, hostile–restrictive, and hostile–permissive. He determined that the warm–permissive quadrant contained the most positive characteristics.

How can one reconcile the fact that in Baldwin's (1948) work control was positive, whereas in Becker's (1964) work permissiveness was more desirable? One way is to note that in Becker's work restrictiveness included two issues: the degree to which rules and regulations existed and the degree to which these were "strictly reinforced." It is likely that Becker's negative findings reflect the fact that he was conflating two dimensions, one related to having rules, and the other to administering those rules in a controlling (or undemocratic) manner. The fact that the dimension picked up rules conveyed in a controlling manner was likely responsible for the negative findings. By contrast, Baldwin separated out having rules and limits from parents' general styles of democratic or undemocratic parenting.

BAUMRIND'S TYPOLOGICAL CONCEPTUALIZATION

In her highly influential early work on parental authority with children Diana Baumrind (Baumrind, 1967, 1977) took a typological approach, dividing parents into different categories. She initially described three patterns of parental authority based on a cluster analysis of 50 behavior ratings of parent interviews and home observations: permissive, authoritarian, and authoritative (see Table 1.1). The *authoritarian* parent attempts to shape, control, and evaluate the child using set standards. He or she values obedience first and foremost and uses forceful measures to inculcate desired behavior. This parent does not encourage verbal give and take but prefers that the child accept his or her word for what is right. This type of parent tends to enforce rules firmly, confronts and sanctions negative behavior on the part of the child, and discourages independence and individuality. He or she also tends to be rejecting, although Baumrind did identify some authoritarian parents who were less so.

The *authoritative* parent, on the other hand, attempts to direct the child in a rational, issue-oriented manner. He or she encourages verbal give and take, provides reasons for her decisions, and solicits the child's opinions. This parent, like the authoritarian parent, firmly enforces rules and is willing to confront misbehavior, yet, in contrast, he or she encourages independence and individuality.

TABLE 1.1

Baumrind's Patterns of Child Rearing

Pattern	Enforces Rules/ Makes Maturity Demands	Encourages Individuality/ Give and Take
Authoritarian	Yes	No
Authoritative	Yes	Yes
Permissive	No	Yes

The permissive parent is nonpunitive, accepts the child's impulses, and is unlikely to intervene by curbing them. He or she also responds to the child in an affirmative way. This parent imposes few demands, and thus the child has few household responsibilities. The permissive parent does not enforce rules firmly and tends to ignore or excuse misbehavior but, like the authoritative parent, encourages independence and individuality.

Baumrind and Black (1967) examined the consequences of these parenting patterns for children in preschool. In a follow-up study, Baumrind (1977) evaluated the children when they were 8 and 9 years old. She found that the preschool children of authoritarian parents were moody and unhappy, relatively aimless, and did not get along well with other children. By ages 8 and 9, these same children, particularly the boys, were low in achievement motivation and social assertion.

In contrast, the preschool children of authoritative parents were energetic, socially outgoing, and independent. The 8- and 9-year-olds were highly achievement oriented, friendly, and socially responsive.

Finally, the preschool children of permissive parents lacked impulse control and were self-centered and low in achievement motivation. By ages 8 and 9 they were described as low in both social and cognitive competence.

Using this same sample of parents and children, Baumrind (1996) later reframed her views of parenting. She used a two-dimensional conceptualization, that included demandingness and responsiveness. She defined *demandingness* as the "claims parents make on the child to become integrated into the family whole by making maturity demands, supervision, disciplinary efforts and willingness to confront the child who disobeys" (p. 411). Thus, demanding parents supervise and monitor their children and are willing to openly confront them when there is a disagreement or wrongdoing. They expect children to perform up to their abilities and to contribute to the family. She defined *responsiveness* as the extent to which parents "intentionally foster individuality, self-regulation, and self-assertion by being attuned, supportive and acquiescent to the children's special needs and desires" (p. 410). The responsivity dimension thus combined warm supportiveness with valuing and promoting individuality through open give and take.

In Baumrind's (1991a) scheme, parents can be divided into four types: *authoritative* (demanding and responsive), *authoritarian* (demanding but not responsive), *permissive* (more responsive than demanding), and *rejecting/neglecting* (neither responsive nor demanding). When Baumrind examined how children of parents placed into these categories fared, she found the best outcomes for children of authoritative parents and the worst for the rejecting/neglecting parents.

When the children were approximately 15 years old, Baumrind (1991b) conducted another follow-up, this time dividing the parents into six types. She further differentiated the *demanding–responsive* parents in a way that was particularly relevant to parenting in adolescence. First, she distinguished parents who were authoritative (demanding and responsive) from those who were *directive* (valuing conformity above individuality and high in demandingness). The directive parents were further divided into *intrusive* and *nonintrusive* types (*authoritarian–directive* and *nonauthoritarian directive*, respectively). There were two types of permissive parents: Those who were highly committed to their children were labeled *democratic*, and those who were not as committed were labeled *nondirective*. A *good enough* group was characterized by medium low to medium high demandingness but only moderate supportiveness. Finally, an *unengaged* group did not structure or monitor their children and was highly disorganized.

Comparing the children of these different groups, Baumrind (1991b) found that adolescents of authoritative and democratic parents were high in competence, individuation, maturity, achievement motivation, and self-regulation. Children of directive parents lacked individuation and autonomy and were rated high in seeking adult approval but low in achievement. The low drug use of these adolescents, combined with their low achievement, suggests that although they were conforming, they lacked initiative. Adolescents from nondirective homes were low in achievement orientation, competence, and self-regulation and engaged in more drug use than those from directive homes. Children from unengaged families exhibited the poorest outcomes, including high externalizing behavior, drug and alcohol use, and low achievement.

Following up on this work, Dornbusch, Ritter, Leiderman, Roberts, and Fraleigh (1987) asked whether parenting typologies could predict behavior patterns in adolescents. They devised a questionnaire about parents that was completed by a diverse group of almost 8,000 adolescents. Their results supported Baumrind's (1967, 1977) findings with younger children: Adolescent children of parents who were less permissive, less authoritarian, and more authoritative performed better in school.

Similarly, Steinberg, Mounts, Lamborn, and Dornbusch (1991) had adolescents from a variety of backgrounds describe their parents using three dimensions. The first was acceptance (e.g., "I can count on [my mother] to help me if I have a problem"). The second was firm control (e.g., "How much do your parents really know what you do in your free time?"), and the third was psychological autonomy (e.g., "How often do your parents tell you their ideas are correct and that you should not question them?", "When you get a poor grade in school, do your parents try to make your life miserable?"). Parents rated high on the three dimensions were identified as authoritative. These were the parents whose children had better grades and experienced less psychological distress; the children also showed more self-reliance and less delinquency.

UNPACKING AUTHORITATIVE PARENTING: PSYCHOLOGICAL CONTROL VERSUS PSYCHOLOGICAL AUTONOMY

Steinberg (1990) reasoned that although the positive effects of authoritative parenting were compelling, it was important to know which aspects of this typology were most influential in creating positive outcomes for children. He suggested that authoritative parenting combined acceptance, psychological autonomy or democracy, and behavioral control. Steinberg's differentiation between psychological and behavioral control represented an important advance. Psychological control stifles children's expressions of autonomy and independent initiations; behavioral control concerns the presence of rules and regulations.

In studying these three dimensions, Steinberg, Elmen, and Mounts (1989) used the Child Report of Parental Behavior Inventory (Schaefer, 1965b), which identified three parenting dimensions: psychological autonomy versus psychological control, firm control, and acceptance. The Psychological Control scale had subscales such as intrusiveness, parental direction, and control through guilt. The dimension of psychological control to psychological autonomy focused on the covert psychological methods of controlling a child's activities as well as behaviors that would not permit the child to develop as an individual apart from the family. The concept includes affect-laden expressions, criticisms, and excessive personal control. Firm control, on the other hand, referred to monitoring and limit setting.

Steinberg, Elmen, and Mounts (1989) found that each aspect of authoritative parenting—acceptance, psychological autonomy, and behavioral control—contributed independently to school achievement in teens. They found that these aspects affected school achievement by facilitating adolescents' psychosocial maturity, including positive work orientation, self-reliance, and self-esteem.

Barber (1996) also separated out the effects of different dimensions. He defined *psychological control* as attempts that "intrude into the psychological and emotional development of the child" and *behavioral control* as "attempts to manage or control the child's behavior." He hypothesized that psychological control would be associated with adolescents' internalizing symptoms, such as depression and withdrawal. Lack of behavioral control, on the other hand, would undermine the development of the children's capacities to regulate their own behavior. This would be associated with externalizing symptomatology. Barber found support for these hypotheses in studies that used children's reports, parents' reports, and observations of interactions between parents and children.

CONTROL IN BAUMRIND'S STUDIES: CONFUSION AND A RECONCILIATION

In 1981 Catherine Lewis published a critique of Baumrind's work in the journal *Psychological Bulletin*. She argued that there is an inherent conflict between Baumrind's notion that control is positive for children's adjustment and attribution theory, which stresses that functionally superfluous control undermines children's taking on behaviors in the absence of adult surveillance.

Baumrind (1983), in her spirited reply to Lewis, argued that firm control is not equivalent to functionally superfluous control; rather, firm control is what one sees when parents make age-appropriate demands on children, for example, to do chores, to help themselves to breakfast, to follow through on what is asked of them. Parents high in firm control effectively follow through in conveying their wishes to their children. Whether that control is applied in a way that is facilitative or undermining of children's autonomy depends on whether it is embedded within an authoritarian or authoritative configuration. In fact, although Baumrind strongly believed in the configural analysis and did not make direct comparisons between parents high in firm control who are and are not directive, she did state that she doubts that "in the absence of warmth and inductive reasoning, firm control is linearly related to internalization" (p. 133). In short, there is no conflict between the parenting characteristics Baumrind advocates; firm control does not imply a directive approach.

What can we conclude from this review of the literature? If we interpret *control* as meaning having control, being an authority (not permissive), making age-appropriate demands (having firm control), setting limits, and monitoring children's behavior (behavioral control), then we find a clear consensus that children do better when parents are "in control." Children need rules, guidelines, and limits for optimal development. Baumrind's (1967, 1977) work has shown that children of permissive parents lacked self-control and self-reliance, and that the children were immature. B. K. Barber (1996) found more disruptive, acting-out behavior from children of parents low in behavioral control.

On the other hand, if we interpret *control* as meaning controlling children—in other words, placing paramount value on compliance, pressuring children toward specified outcomes, and discouraging verbal give-and-take and discussion, as opposed to supporting children's initiations, providing reasons, and respecting children's viewpoints—we find a clear, yet opposite, consensus that control has negative consequences for children.

All of this seems to ring true intuitively. But why the consensus? In studying good parenting, we need a perspective from which to understand the effects of the parental environment. Self-determination theory provides such a perspective and explains why control is so problematic for children's development.

2

Fulfilling Children's Needs: The Self-Determination View

When Jamie came home from school that day, she turned down her usual snack. Her mother was puzzled, especially when Jamie dragged herself up to her room and opened up her school books without even being asked. "Something the matter?" her mother asked.

"Nothing. I'm fine," Jamie said.

By dinner, Jamie's glumness affected everyone. When she knocked over her glass of milk, she burst into tears and ran up to her bed, sobbing.

Her mother patted her back until Jamie finally told her. "Recess was terrible! Sarah and Callie said I couldn't play with them. They wouldn't talk to me all day long!"

Jamie's mother agonized over her daughter's misery. Finally, she crept downstairs to call Sarah's mother. "We need a way to fix this problem," Jamie's mother said.

But instead of everything being neatly ironed out, Jamie's mother noticed that Jamie's friends stopped calling her. Jamie didn't ask for play dates. Instead of fixing a small problem, the parental intervention exacerbated the situation.

One way to think about the issue of controlling children is to begin with the perspective of the child. What is the child's nature, and how does that nature determine what is effective parenting?

Self-determination theory, which begins with the concept of human beings as active and agentic, addresses this very issue. Humans engage their surroundings in an attempt to master them, pursue the things they love, and persist in goal-directed behavior. Think of the curiosity of infants in observing what is around them, first with their eyes, then their hands and mouths. We do not have to teach children to be active and curious. It is their nature.

Harry Harlow, the primate psychologist, coined the term *intrinsic motivation* to explain the behavior of monkeys who, in his laboratory, explored mazes just for the sake of doing so and would even forgo food to continue exploring them (Harlow, Harlow, & Meyer, 1950). This is a perfect example of how satisfying learning can be. Intrinsic motivation refers to the motivation for activities that we pursue for their own sake—for the inherent enjoyment and positive feelings we get when we do them. According to Deci (1975), humans are born with innate energy to grow and develop, to increase their skills, and to master their worlds. This intrinsic motivation is the energy source that underlies such spontaneous activity as exploration and persistence.[1]

A key part of this theory is that underlying intrinsic motivation are three psychological needs:

- The need to feel autonomous
- The need to feel competent
- The need to feel related to those around us

People are born with these needs and are most likely to be intrinsically motivated when these needs are satisfied. Let's take a look at each of these needs.

First we discuss autonomy. deCharms (1968), using Heider's (1958) notion of "perceived locus of causality," argued that humans need to feel that their actions emanate from themselves. In other words, they need to experience an internal locus of causality for the regulation of their behavior. deCharms described the experience of being an "origin," or initiator of behavior. That is in contrast to the experience of being a "pawn," one who feels pushed around by the surrounding environment. When we feel that our behaviors stem from ourselves, we feel like agents. We feel free. We feel as if we have choice, and we are intrinsically motivated to pursue activities.

---

[1]It is important to point out that there is a controversy over the existence of intrinsic motivation. Behaviorists, for example, believe that all behavior is under the control of contingencies—that is, rewards and punishments—in the environment. Such theorists would argue that, if behaviors appear to be done for their own sake, without a separable reward, then the observer simply does not yet know what contingencies are controlling the behavior. In response to such critiques self-determination theorists make several counterarguments. First, monkeys, rats, and other animals will *forgo* food (a reinforcer) and endure shock (a punishment) to explore novel areas (Deci & Ryan, 1985b). This refutes the idea that such exploration can be explained by its pairing with some reinforcer. Second, children engage in exploration and play from birth, before they have the opportunity to learn that such behaviors lead to rewards or punishments. Still, behavioral theorists have offered several alternative ways to understand the results of studies conducted on intrinsic motivation. I discuss such ways in chapter 4 in the section on rewards.

Imagine the activities in our adult lives that are intrinsically motivated. These are activities that we choose to pursue because they are fun or interesting. Such activities might include reading, swimming, writing, or talking with a friend. When we engage in these activities we do not feel compelled or pressured—the initiation and the regulation of the activity come from within us. We engage in these activities willingly and freely, without pressures to pursue them. Csikszentmihalyi (1990) described such activities as *flow*, because they involve intense concentration and de-emphasis of time. He found that, when asked about activities that involved flow, most adults nominated leisure activities, although they also frequently listed work as well.

A second need underlying intrinsic motivation is the need to feel competent or effective in interacting with the environment. R. White (1959) described a motivation to be effective as an inherent motivation. When we feel competent, we are motivated to continue. We persist. The experience of incompetence, on the other hand, undermines intrinsic motivation. We simply don't want to continue doing that at which we feel incompetent.

The third fundamental need is for relatedness. As Harlow (1958) argued, individuals need to experience love and interpersonal contact to develop optimally. We need warmth and affection. Similarly, Bowlby (1969) emphasized the importance of children feeling a sense of security from their parents. Considerable research on attachment (e.g., Ainsworth, Blehar, Waters, & Wall, 1978) has demonstrated that if infants do not experience security in their primary relationships, their exploratory activity diminishes, and various adjustment problems are likely to follow. In this sense, intrinsic motivation flourishes only when there is a backdrop of relatedness to others.

Thus, in intrinsic motivation, the active tendency to master, to be curious, and to be active in the environment is based on the satisfaction of these innate needs. A corollary of this theory, and one most relevant to our discussion, is that when the environment supports a person's innate needs for autonomy, competence, and relatedness, then motivation, adjustment, and well-being result. In contrast, environments that undermine the fulfillment of those needs result in a lack of motivation and feelings of ill-being. Three dimensions of the environment facilitate these innate needs:

- Autonomy support versus control
- Involvement
- Structure

The first of these, autonomy support versus control, concerns the degree to which the environment allows individuals to feel that they initiate their actions, rather than feel that they are being coerced. Characteristics of environments that provide that feeling—thus supporting autonomy—include the ability to choose, opportunities to solve problems on one's own, and minimal pressure to behave in a certain way. Each of these characteristics help people feel that they are the ones originating their actions.

Conversely, people feel controlled when they perceive strong pressures to behave, whether in the form of evaluation, deadlines, guilt inducement, or other contingencies. Each of these leads people to feel pushed or coerced, which undermines their feeling that they are initiating their own actions. Consider the example at the beginning of this chapter. When Jamie's mother intervenes in her dilemma by calling the other mothers, she attempts to solve Jamie's problem for her. Jamie feels like a pawn in the situation—hardly an active role.

The autonomy supportive versus controlling nature of the environment can refer to many aspects of the environment, including the physical layout. For example, when an area is so crowded that a person has only one direction in which he or she can move, that restriction controls one's movement. However, clearly the most salient and important aspects of the environment are the interpersonal ones—the ways other people treat us. Although the topic of this book is the way in which parents support or control children, autonomy support and control issues are not reserved for parenting. These can be characteristic of any interpersonal environment. Does a teacher provide options for a topic to be pursued? Does a doctor use pressure and scare tactics to induce patients to quit smoking? Does a spouse insist on just one way in which to solve a problem with a friend?

Researchers have described the autonomy supportive versus controlling orientation of the environment provided by teachers (e.g., Deci, Nezlek, & Sheinman, 1981), work managers (Deci, Connell, & Ryan, 1989), physicians (Williams, Rodin, Ryan, Grolnick, & Deci, 1998), and coaches. Thus, the concept of autonomy support is a general rubric for an orientation to interacting with others, whereas the content of what may be considered autonomy supportive varies for different individuals, developmental levels, and settings. This is also true for parenting. For a young infant, autonomy support may be provided in the experience of the baby being able to use his or her hands freely rather than being pulled to touch something. For a preschool child, it may be a choice between two outfits. For an adolescent, it may be having a say in the decision of which college to attend. The advantage of such a global approach is that, although the nature of autonomy support and control can differ at different developmental periods or in different contexts, the concept remains consistent. Thus, we can begin to ask questions about the importance of, or continuity of, autonomy support to control at different developmental levels without becoming stuck on the problem of differences over time in the content of specific parental behaviors.

Autonomy supportive events can be defined as those that lead a person to experience his or her behavior as initiated from within, or to have an internal locus of causality for the behavior. By contrast, controlling events lead a person to feel like his or her behavior is being initiated from without, or to have an external locus of causality. Definitions of autonomy support and control thus focus on the experience of the individual and the resulting locus of causality. This focus takes into account that objectively similar events may have different effects on different people. Individuals can experience the same environment differently; thus, it is not the objective quality of the environment but rather the "functional significance" of the environment that makes it controlling or autonomous. To be sure, in some extreme environments, such as a concentration camp, everyone would experience control. However, in more ambiguous or less constrained situations, this may not be the case.

One study of classroom environments, for example (Ryan & Grolnick, 1986), revealed wide variations within any classroom in the degree to which the teacher was described as controlling or autonomy supportive. Another study found that children who described their teachers as controlling were those who had controlling parents (Grolnick, 1987). To be sure, the different ways the same teacher's behavior is described may be the result of the fact that teachers probably do treat different children differently. Children probably "pull" a similar level of control from parents and teachers by their own behavior as well. However, even beyond this, it is also likely that children interpret the same behaviors as affording autonomy or control and are thus affected by them differently. As a college professor, I hear students comment about the same professors being controlling or autonomy supportive on the basis of listening to the same large lectures. I am also aware that my students interpret my behavior in very different ways. The differential functional significance of the same behaviors is an important point and one I discuss when I take up the issue of control in various contexts.

What evidence is there that the controlling versus autonomy supportive nature of the environment is important to children's motivation? In our first parenting study, we (Grolnick, Frodi, & Bridges, 1984) studied mothers with 1-year-olds. We gave mothers two toys to play with on the floor with their infants. The mothers were given the ambiguous instruction to "sit next to your child while he (she) plays with the toy." We then videotaped the dyads playing for 3 minutes. Some mothers took the ambiguous instruction to mean "I must make sure my child does this right." They spent the three minutes firing instructions: "Put the block in; no, not THERE, THERE!" They became critical and serious.

Other mothers interpreted the same instruction to mean that they should be a resource for their children. They let the children explore and problem solve, and they were available if difficulties arose. We rated the mothers in terms of how supportive of the children's autonomy or controlling the mothers were. Autonomy supportive mothers followed their children, provided encouragement, and gave just enough assistance to get their children back on track if they were tripped up. Controlling mothers tended to lead the interaction, telling the child what to do and doing more than was needed.

We then gave children interesting tasks to do—without the assistance of their mothers—and watched to see whether the children would persist or give up. The findings were striking: The children of mothers who were more controlling when interacting with them tended to persist less and give up more easily when on their own, whereas the children of the more autonomy supportive mothers tended to persist and tried to solve the problems presented by the toys. It seems that the pushy, pressuring behavior of the mothers undermined the children's own motivation. When given opportunities to explore and master, those children tended to lose interest and give up.

Deci, Driver, Hotchkiss, Robbins, and Wilson (1993) found similar results in a group of 5- to 7-year olds. They reported that mothers who, during a play session, were rated as being relatively controlling had children whose subsequent intrinsic motivation (i.e., involvement with similar toys when given choices of several toys with which to play) was lower than those whose vocalizations were rated as more autonomy supportive.

However, autonomy support is not the only dimension that is necessary to facilitate motivation and adjustment. Recall that I discussed three innate needs underlying intrinsic motivation: autonomy, competence, and relatedness. It is crucial that the environment support needs for competence and relatedness by providing structure and involvement, particularly in regard to motivation for nonintrinsically motivated behaviors, which I discuss later.

I have defined *involvement* as the provision of resources by the parent to the child. Resources can be in the form of time devoted to the child; more tangible resources, such as the provision of books necessary for school; or more emotional resources, such as warmth and availability. Furthermore, involvement includes taking an interest in the child's activities and world and knowing what is going on in them. When parents and children have a shared understanding about what happens on a day-to-day basis, their sense of connection and relatedness are enhanced.

Grolnick and Slowiaczek (1994) stressed that involvement is better seen as a domain specific concept rather than a global one. Parents can choose—or, because of demands placed on them, be forced—to be involved in different areas of their children's lives. Thus a parent can be highly involved in a child's school life but less so in the child's sports. These differences result from parents' values or priorities in an environment that forces them to allocate scarce resources.

Beyond involvement is the importance of structure in children's lives. *Structure* refers to the provision of guidelines and information that children need so they can be self-determining. This involves communicating expectations to children, explaining why these expectations are important, delineating the consequences of meeting or not meeting these expectations, and consistently following through. This dimension is parallel to what I discussed earlier as Steinberg's (1990) notion of behavioral control, or Baumrind's (1967) construct of firm control. Structure could, for example, involve providing a rationale for a request, such as explaining how a playmate might feel if the child grabbed a toy away from him or her. It also involves ensuring that the requested action is appropriate for the child's cognitive and emotional capabilities.

As the parenting literature indicates, the tendency to confuse structure and control is widespread. An example may help convey this difference. Imagine establishing a specific time when a child should come inside from playing outdoors. One approach, which involves a high level of structure, would be for the parent to provide information about when the child needs to be home. The child may be told that when the clock's little hand is on the 5, that is the time that he or she must come inside. The child may also be told that he or she will get one reminder about when that time arrives. If this has been a problem in the past, the parent may even let the child know the consequences of needing to be reminded more than twice. Perhaps the child will have to come in tomorrow when the little hand is on the 4. All of this can be conceived as structure. However, the same level of structure can be communicated in a way that is either controlling or autonomy supportive. For example, the controlling version would be for the parent to give this information with "shoulds," threats, and excess pressure, all the while reminding the child that he or she will be watched. On the other hand, the parent can give this information in a way that conveys the parent's understanding that the child would like to play longer, with a rationale for why it is important to come in, leaving off the controlling locution.

In a study with older children designed to examine all three parenting dimensions, Richard Ryan and I interviewed 114 parents—64 mothers and 50 fathers—of elementary-age children (Grolnick & Ryan, 1989). The interview focused on how these parents motivated school and home behaviors and how they reacted when the child did well or poorly at carrying out these behaviors. The behaviors were those that are not naturally fun for children: doing homework, going to bed on time, brushing teeth, cleaning their rooms.

Some parents were rated as high on autonomy support. They communicated in the interview that they valued their child's display of independent thoughts and actions versus feeling that the child should never question authority. In line with this, they tended to use autonomy-oriented parenting techniques, such as discussion and providing rules in an autonomy-supportive manner by involving the children in decision making. They relied less on controlling, power assertive methods such as physical punishment and bribes. For example, one parent, rated as highly controlling, told us that every evening she stood over her child to make sure he completed his homework. Another parent, rated as more autonomy supportive, clearly communicated to her child the consequences of incomplete homework but allowed the child to make choices with regard to accomplishing the task.

Parents who were rated as highly involved tended to know a great deal about their children. When we interviewed them about school, they were able to tell us their child's favorite and least favorite subjects. They asked about their child's school day and made a point of trying to spend time with their child. It is interesting that involved parents were not necessarily *in the home* more hours than less involved parents but, when they were home, they spent more time in shared activities.

We also saw the extremes of structured and unstructured parenting. In more structured homes there were rules and expectations, some of which were stated, some just understood. In these homes parents consistently enforced these rules and guidelines. In unstructured homes there was a great deal of chaos and disorganization. For example, in one home the parents had no rules for when homework should be done. Because of their disorganization, they frequently made it impossible for the child to begin homework before a reasonable bedtime, which also was not definitely stated.

Our findings, depicted in Table 2.1, suggested that children whose parents were more supportive of autonomy were more self-regulated in school (i.e., they reported more autonomous regulation of school activities; Grolnick & Ryan, 1989). Furthermore, children whose parents were more autonomy supportive acted up less in the classroom, according to teachers. They seemed to take more responsibility for their behavior both at home and at school. They also performed better in school and had higher achievement scores and grades.

We also observed important effects of level of structure in the home (Grolnick & Ryan, 1989). When clear and consistent guidelines were available, children felt more in control in school. They seemed to have the sense that there were predictable consequences to their actions. If they tried hard in school, they would do well. When homes were less structured, children thought their own worlds might be more haphazard and weren't sure how to make success happen for themselves.

Finally, I present a theme that will run throughout this book: Involvement was extremely important in children's adjustment. The more involved parents were, the better the children did in school, and the fewer problems they had.

TABLE 2.1

Relations Between Parenting and Children's Competence Outcomes

Outcome	Autonomy Support	Involvement	Structure
Motivation			
Self-regulation	7.65***	—	—
Control understanding	—	5.14**	16.22***
Perceived competence	—	—	—
Teacher Ratings			
Acting out	11.67**	—	—
Competence	16.14***	—	—
Achievement			
Achievement	6.54**	6.29**	—
Grades	5.43**	—	—

*$p < .05$, **$p < .01$, ***$p < .001$, — means nonsignificant findings.

Studies such as the ones just discussed underscore the idea that when parents support children's autonomy they facilitate children's motivation to master their environments. They also increase children's sense of competence and their control over their worlds, and they increase children's ability to regulate their own behavior. Conversely, parenting styles that control children's behavior induce children to feel that their successes and failures are in the hands of others rather than their own and undermine children's motivation and feelings of competence. These effects are apparent as early as 1 year of age.

AUTONOMY SUPPORT TO CONTROL AND RELATIONSHIPS

I have provided evidence that control is detrimental to children's intrinsic motivation and thus problematic for children's feelings of mastery and persistence in solving problems on their own. The use of controls in situations where children are naturally inclined clearly undermines parents' goals and is one way that control backfires. In this section I discuss another way that controls backfire, in terms of the parent–child relationship.

How do parents conceptualize their relationships with their children? To answer this question, Harach and Kuczynski (1999) asked 24 mothers and 24 fathers of 4- to 7-year-olds to spontaneously define the parent–child relationship. They categorized parents' spontaneous descriptions into definitions that involved *vertical* notions, such as authority and influence (i.e., parent as teacher or protector), and notions that were *horizontal*. Horizontal notions involved symmetrical notions, such as friendship and companionship and intimacy and closeness. Harach and Kuczynski's results showed that horizontal themes of friendship and intimacy were strongly present in parents' descriptions. It was clear that the parents thought of their children in terms other than simply power ones; they thought of them as friends and companions as well. Parents' goals for their children were not simply compliance; they also desired a positive and close relationship.

I suggest that autonomy support facilitates not only motivation but also feelings of closeness and relatedness. Many researchers have found that when experimenters act in an autonomy supportive versus a controlling manner, children enjoy tasks more and feel less pressure and tension while completing them (e.g., Deci, Eghrari, Patrick, & Leone, 1994). Gurland and Grolnick (2000) more directly explored the link between autonomy supportiveness and experience in an interaction. They focused on the development of rapport between children and unfamiliar adults. Children saw videotapes of two adults, each of whom led them through an interesting task (e.g., writing about oneself, drawing an animal). In one of the videotapes the adult was controlling in her style of interacting. For example, she used controlling locution (e.g., "you have to write about yourself"). In the other videotape, the adult used an autonomy supportive style. For example, she avoided controlling locution (e.g., "the task involves writing about yourself") and acknowledged children's feelings about the task (e.g., "I know you might usually like to draw other things, but please draw an animal"). After the simulated interactions, children were asked about their feelings of rapport with the adult (i.e., how much warmth, friendliness, and liking they experienced toward the adult). Although the two adults were equally positive in their affect, children reported greater rapport with the autonomy supportive adult.

The results from studies with parents also point to the importance of autonomy support for relationships. For example, Avery and Ryan (1988) asked children to describe how autonomy supportive versus controlling their parents were in interacting with them. They were also asked to complete a projective task in which their representations of their parents were coded. The more autonomy supportive children described their parents as, the more nurturant parents were depicted in the children's descriptions. This study suggests that autonomy support facilitates feelings of connectedness and closeness with parents. Given that intimacy and relatedness are clearly qualities of the parent–child relationship that parents value highly, control can be seen as not only undermining children's motivation but also as having unwanted side effects for the parent–child relationship.

When Jamie's mother takes Jamie's friendship dilemma into her own hands and takes responsibility for solving her problem, Jamie feels both controlled and incompetent. Her mother's behavior makes it less likely that Jamie will be able to solve problems like this on her own in the future. Over time, the use of such controlling techniques can have a profound impact on Jamie's motivation and self-regulation. It may also affect her feelings about sharing personal information with her mother. But Jamie's mother only wanted to help—should she have stayed out of the situation altogether? This question brings up the topic of involvement and its interplay with autonomy support. I take up this issue in the next chapter.

3

The Complexity of Control: Disentangling Parenting Dimensions

One of the more pleasant rituals in the Cunningham household has father and daughter riding their bikes together to and from school everyday. One hectic morning Lauren, 9, couldn't find her helmet and wore an old, funny-shaped one she found in the back of the closet. As they were tucking their bikes into the school's rack, Bob Cunningham noticed a girl who he knew had been bothering Lauren all year standing and staring at them.

"Lauren, everybody's laughing at you," the girl said.

Lauren looked stricken.

Bob went into protective mode. He pulled the child aside. "That was a very mean thing to say," he said to the little girl. The girl shrugged and walked away.

"Father!" Lauren said, embarrassed, and turned away herself.

For the rest of the day, Bob Cunningham felt terrible. Taking the reins hadn't solved anything for his daughter. It had probably made things worse. Lauren hadn't learned any new tricks in negotiating the treacherousness of bullies. In fact, by taking over in this situation, Bob had only alienated his own daughter.

In the three parenting dimensions we have looked at so far—autonomy support, structure, and involvement—we have seen some compelling evidence regarding the negative effects of control. Now let us look at controversies about involvement and structure. I believe these can be reconciled using the concept of control.

22

CONTROL VERSUS INVOLVEMENT:
CLARIFYING THE ISSUES

First, although the term *involvement* has a positive connotation in the research world, which is obvious from the vast literature on parent involvement in children's schooling, the term actually has many meanings. Often when I have discussed the concept of controlling parents, friends have said to me "Oh, you mean overinvolved parents." The term *overinvolvement* implies that involvement, at its extremes, can be bad for children. We think of the negative stereotype of the "soccer mom" who centers her life around her children and is around 100% of the time. How can we reconcile that concept with the idea of being controlling? How do we come to see involvement as negative? I argue that the concept of involvement has been conflated with control, and that has led to confusing findings.

A prime example is the notion of enmeshed families in the family therapy literature. *Enmeshment* refers to a dysfunctional family system characterized by high involvement, poor boundaries, and a lack of differentiation and of individual autonomy. Families like these, the literature suggests, lead individuals to be poorly adjusted and to have psychosomatic symptoms (Minuchin, 1974). Olsen, Sprenkle, and Russell (1979) operationalized Minuchin's (1974) scheme of family functioning. In the Family Adaptability and Cohesion Evaluation Scales (FACES) and numerous revisions, they proposed that families could be evaluated along two salient dimensions: cohesion and adaptability. *Cohesion* refers to the degree of closeness among family members and the degree of autonomy a person experiences in the family system. The FACES treats cohesion as one dimension, with extreme overinvolvement or enmeshment at one end and extreme underinvolvement or disengagement at the other. Using this scale, several researchers have asked: Are moderate levels of cohesion optimal?

The answer seems to be no. Chapin (1989) found that family disengagement was negatively related to adolescent grades; however, adolescents from enmeshed families had scores that were significantly higher than adolescents from "optimally cohesive" (mid-range) families. Similarly, in a study of 80 high school students, Kersey and Protinsky (1987) found that students who scored in the enmeshed category of cohesion on the FACES II (Olsen et al., 1985) had higher adjustment scores on the Offer Self-Image Questionnaire (Offer, Ostros, & Howard, 1981).

How can these discomfiting results be explained? Beavers and Voeller (1983) criticized Olsen et al. (1979) for linking and confounding cohesion—a variable that defines the interaction among family members—with autonomy—a developmental concept that concerns the functioning of the self. Enmeshment is conceptually defined by two conditions: high closeness and involvement and a lack of individual autonomy. To define enmeshment both in terms of lack of autonomy and high closeness is to confuse the two issues.

Such arguments hark back to the re-examination of these concepts in the literature on adolescence. Whereas early studies focused on the needs of teenagers to sever the bond with their parents and become independent (e.g., Blos, 1962), more recent views stress that optimal development is fostered not by detachment but by becoming more self-reliant in the context of attachment to family members. Thus, attachment and autonomy are defined as separate and related dimensions, both crucial for adolescent development (Ryan & Lynch, 1989).

DISENTANGLING INVOLVEMENT
AND AUTONOMY SUPPORT

To look at whether very high levels of parental involvement are beneficial for children, it is important to separate out the amount and quality of that involvement. One study from Steinberg's laboratory and two studies from my own have examined the interplay of involvement and control.

Steinberg, Lamborn, Dornbusch, and Darling (1992) asked whether parental authoritativeness would moderate the impact of parental involvement or parental encouragement on adolescent achievement. In particular, they suggested that parent involvement would be least correlated with academic achievement when the home environment was least authoritative. Although there were correlations between involvement and performance across all groups, the weakest relations were observed for the nonauthoritative group. Thus, there is some evidence that, at least for children's grades, any amount of involvement is positive and better than none. Still, controlling behavior can somewhat undermine the beneficial effects of involvement.

As part of our longitudinal work on parent involvement, a study conducted by my research group (Grolnick, Gehl, & Manzo, 1997; Benjet, 1995) looked at both the amount and quality of parents' involvement in their children's schooling and found that the effect of these different constructs depended on what outcomes were looked at. A diverse sample of 209 mothers, their children, and their children's teachers participated. We assessed parent involvement (school, cognitive, and personal) using parent, teacher, and child ratings. We also assessed children's experiences of that involvement from positive to negative (e.g., "I feel good when my mother talks to my teacher," "I don't like to talk about what happens at school with my mother").

It was the controlling nature of their parents' involvement that made the children feel negatively about this involvement. Indeed, the children who saw their parents as autonomy supportive tended to be positive about their parents' involvement, whereas children who saw their parents as controlling tended to be more negative about their parents' involvement. The relative importance of each of the two dimensions—level of involvement and quality of involvement—depended on the outcomes examined. For grades, level of involvement was key; parents who were more involved had children who were doing better in school. This held for any kind of involvement. For motivation, however, the quality of that involvement was key. Regardless of level of involvement, autonomy support was associated with more autonomous motivation. Thus, involvement may give children the resources they need to do well, but it does not assure autonomous motivation. There was one interaction between level and quality of involvement for perceived competence: For children in the high-involvement group, quality did not matter; for children in the low-involvement group, perceived competence was higher if the quality was positive.

What does this mean? The effects of involvement and autonomy support were different. Involvement assured higher grades, but not autonomous motivation, while autonomy support facilitated a sense of autonomy, but did not necessarily result in the child doing well. The best outcomes were in the high autonomy support, high involvement group.

Weiss and Grolnick (1991) focused on adolescents in the 7th through 11th grades who reported on parental involvement and autonomy support. They also filled out the Achenbach Youth Self-Report (Achenbach, 1991) in which they rated their own internalizing (e.g., depression) and externalizing (e.g., acting out) symptomatology. We divided parents into three groups: the most involved, which comprised the top 15%; the middle 70%; and the least involved, or the bottom 15%. We found that for both externalizing and internalizing symptoms involvement and autonomy support had an effect. Specifically, the high-involvement group and the high autonomy support group both reported the fewest internalizing and externalizing symptoms. There were also significant interactions for both types of symptoms, indicating that the combination of high involvement and low autonomy support yielded a high level of symptoms. In some cases, these were higher than those for the low-involvement group. These interaction effects are illustrated in Figures 3.1 and 3.2. When parents are involved in an autonomy supportive manner, that involvement is associated with a variety of desirable child outcomes. When they are involved in a controlling way, however, the involvement can have a deleterious effect on child outcomes.

Can parents display too much involvement, warmth, or caring? Should parents stay away from swim meets, soccer games, and friendship dilemmas? The answer to this, I think, is a qualified no. There can be too much involvement only when that involvement undermines the child's autonomy. Research sup-

Parental Involvement by Autonomy Support

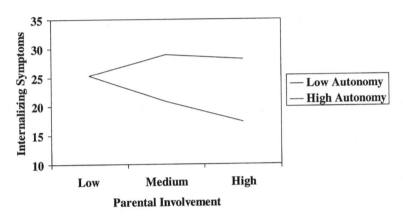

FIG. 3.1.   Parental involvement by autonomy support, internalizing symptoms.

Parental Involvement by Autonomy Support

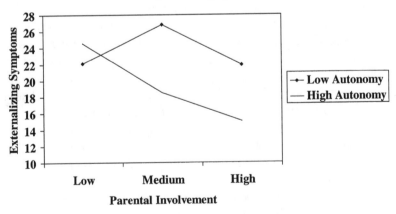

FIG. 3.2.   Parental involvement by autonomy support, externalizing symptoms.

ports the idea that involvement, even—and especially—at its highest ends, gives necessary resources and support to children, enhances their lives, and helps them to accomplish their goals when it is afforded in a way that facilitates a sense of autonomy. Highly involved parents at any age fulfill a sense of security and relatedness that serves children well when that involvement is provided in a way that is not intrusive and does not weaken children's autonomy. In the example at the beginning of the chapter, Bob Cunningham falls into the trap of becoming involved in his daughter's confrontation in a controlling manner. Although he had good intentions, his behavior clearly undermined Lauren's autonomy. Finding a balance between involvement and autonomy support may be tricky for parents, as we see in later chapters, because parents who care intensely about their children and who become highly involved will be those most likely to get "hooked" into focusing on their children's performance. Such a focus may then lead parents to have their own stakes in how well their children perform. As I describe later, such hooks, or ego involvement, in children's outcomes put parents at risk for controlling behavior. It is, however, quite possible to achieve a balance of providing high levels of healthy, autonomy supportive involvement.

STRUCTURE VERSUS CONTROL

The work I reviewed in chapters 1 and 2 suggested that being "in control" is positive for children's development. This has held true for several factors relevant to being in control, such as monitoring (e.g., B. K. Barber, Olsen, & Shagle, 1994; Crouter, MacDermid, McHale, & Perry-Jenkins, 1990; Patterson & Stouthamer-Loeber, 1984), providing rules and guidelines (Grolnick & Ryan, 1989), and maintaining demands or behavioral standards (Baumrind, 1991a). What is of crucial interest here, needless to say, is whether the effects of that structure are always positive or whether, when combined with controllingness, they are undermining of children's motivation.

Pomerantz and Ruble (1998) asked just this question in a study of parents' help with homework in second through fifth graders. They looked at the interplay between exercising control, which I refer to as *structure*, and whether that structure is conveyed in a controlling versus autonomy granting way. Parents filled out a daily checklist assessing their helping, monitoring, decision making, praising, and disciplining in the homework process. They differentiated between behaviors that were controlling versus autonomy granting. One set of controlling behaviors were likely to make a child feel that he or she was being controlled by external forces; for example, when a mother gives her child a reward for doing well in school. The second set of controlling behaviors conveyed that performance was most important: A mother might pick a topic for her child's school assignment. The third set of controlling behaviors communicated that the child was not capable of solving his or her own problems; for example, when a father helps his child without being asked.

Conversely, autonomy granting behaviors were those that were likely to either make a child feel that his or her behavior emanated from within; for example, when a mother attributes good performance in school to the child's ability or to his or her enjoyment of the task. Another type of autonomy granting behavior is when the parent communicates that the child is capable of solving his or her own problems; for example, the child is encouraged to solve his or her own problem when he or she requests help.

The authors then looked at four patterns of help:

1. *Autonomy granting with control*; for example, encouraging the child to do work on his or her own and then providing help.
2. *Controlling alone*; for example, helping immediately when asked.
3. *Autonomy granting alone*; for instance, encouraging the child to do something alone but providing no help.
4. *No response* to a request for help.

The controlling behavior by itself undermined intrinsic motivation, whereas the controlling behavior with autonomy granting was positively associated with intrinsic motivation. Autonomy granting alone had no effect on children.

Pomerantz and Ruble's (1998) results suggest that structuring behaviors are most facilitative when they are combined with autonomy support. Assistance provided in a controlling manner undermined children. In short, these results support the idea that the effects of structuring behaviors depend on the way in which they are conveyed—whether it is in an autonomy-supportive or controlling manner.

Limits—such as not being allowed to jump on the couch, eating food at the table, and keeping glitter from spilling on the floor—are another form of structure. They give children information about the parameters of their situations so that they know what to expect in response to their behavior. We all have to impose limits, but do they necessarily undermine children's intrinsic motivation? Koestner, Ryan, Bernieri, and Holt (1984) examined this question. They looked at the effects of setting limits when it was done in a controlling or noncontrolling context. In the experiment, first- and second-grade children painted pictures. Limits were set in regard to them being neat with the painting materials. The limits were set in either a controlling or a noncontrolling manner. The researchers reasoned that, to relieve the possible controlling pressure created by the existence of limits, it was important to avoid controlling locutions. In a noncontrolling-limits condition they avoided words such as *should* and *must*. They also acknowledged that children might not want to conform to the limits.

After the painting session in which controlling or noncontrolling limits were in effect, Koestner et al. (1984) looked at the intrinsic motivation for painting that the children exhibited, such as whether the children chose to paint when given several alternatives, and the creativity of pictures they created. The authors observed that intrinsic motivation and creativity were undermined by the controlling limits but not by the noncontrolling limits. Thus, again, structure on its own is not undermining of intrinsic motivation—it might, as in Pomerantz and Ruble's (1998) study, be helpful to children. However, its undermining versus facilitating effects depend on whether it is conveyed in a controlling or an autonomy supportive manner. We easily negate our attempts to help when they convey to children messages of incompetence and control.

FURTHER CONTROVERSY: CONTROL AS A DEVELOPMENTAL CONCEPT

Eccles and her colleagues (e.g., Eccles et al., 1993), using person–environment fit theory (Hunt, 1975), have argued that the effects of control depend on the match of the amount of control with the person's subjective needs. If the amount of control provided in the environment matches the person's preferred level of control, there should be positive consequences. Alternatively, if the environment provides more than or less than the desired amount of control, there will be negative consequences.

Eccles and her colleagues (e.g., Eccles & Midgely, 1988; Flanagan, 1985; Mac Iver & Reuman, 1988) addressed this theory in their work on the transition to junior high school. They reasoned that it was likely that, as children got older, they would prefer more participation in decision making in the classroom— their measure of "control" in this instance. They assessed the preferred and actual decision-making opportunities in the classrooms of 2,210 students. As predicted, they found that, relative to sixth graders, seventh graders expressed a greater desire for input into classroom decision making. In contrast, adolescents and teachers reported fewer opportunities for decision making and more regimentation in the seventh-grade classroom (Eccles & Midgley, 1988). Adolescents who experienced their seventh-grade math classrooms as more constraining than their preferred level of participation showed the greatest declines in interest in math (Mac Iver & Reuman, 1988). Eccles and Midgely (1988) found that adolescents who were not given adequate opportunities to participate were most at risk for negative motivational outcomes.

Extensions to the family context support these results. There is an increase from sixth to seventh grade in adolescents' desires to participate in family decision making, and that participation relates to intrinsic school motivation and positive self-esteem (Flanagan, 1985). Furthermore, adolescents who perceived little opportunity to participate meaningfully in family decisions had more conflicts with their parents, relied more on their friends than parents for help with problems, and were more willing to disobey their parents (Fuligni & Eccles, 1990). When opportunities for input increased over time, intrinsic motivation increased. When opportunities decreased over time, intrinsic motivation decreased as well.

So, is it accurate to conclude that controlling behavior is negative only for some individuals at some developmental levels? To date, Eccles and her colleagues have provided compelling evidence that lack of opportunities to participate in decisions (greater control) in young adolescents is undermining of their motivation and of their relationships with their parents. However, the "fit" hypothesis implies that at some developmental levels control has positive sequelae. These authors have not provided evidence that more control is positive at any age, and this is problematic for the "fit" hypothesis. Grolnick et al. (1984) found controlling styles to be undermining as early as 1 year of age. The negative effects of control, however, are probably evident from Day 1. A case in point is Brazelton, Koslowski, and Main's (1974) work on gazing in newborns in which babies whose mothers lead periods of gazing, rather than allowing the child to lead, and who intrude when the child is overloaded with stimulation have shorter and fewer periods of attention over time. Thus, the need to provide responsive parenting, which is sensitive to children's needs for self-regulation, can be seen for Day 1.

Of course, children do change, and it would be unlikely that parenting would not need to adapt to these shifts. One likely area to look for these changes is in optimal levels of structure. Whereas young children require rules, regulations, and guidelines for much of their behavior, older children have a greater capacity to make judgments for themselves and have internalized many of the rules. Parents likely need to lessen the number of rules and give children opportunities to make mistakes. However, this is different than saying that at some points children need control. Rather, children need structure provided in a way that supports their autonomy and provides choice through development. Part of autonomy supportive parenting is taking the child's perspective and being sensitive to his or her desires to solve problems on his or her own. Thus, at different ages, autonomy supportive parenting will look different. For example, at a younger age the control issue might be decision making with regard to two pieces of clothing; at an older age, it might entail a more consequential decision about what courses to take in school. In either case, however, autonomy supportive parenting facilitates the child's sense of being an initiator. Through this style of parenting, children build self-regulation and self-confidence.

CONTROL AS A TECHNIQUE
VERSUS AS A PARENTING CONTEXT

Much of the research on control has focused on discipline. Discipline is clearly an important means by which values are acquired (Grusec & Goodnow, 1994), yet a focus on discipline techniques alone, or on any other specific parenting technique, neglects the idea that these practices occur within an ongoing parent–child relationship and in the context of parents' attitudes toward the child and parenting.

Darling and Steinberg (1993) differentiated between parenting *practices*—the techniques parents use to help them achieve socialization goals— and parenting *style*, which includes attitudes toward the child and the emotional climate in which the parent's behavior is expressed. As such, the term *parenting styles* describes parent–child interaction across a wide range of situations rather than domain-specific techniques. The parenting style involves a relationship between parent and child, which may involve respect or a lack of respect for the child. It can be warm and connected, or it can be disengaged. It can coerce the child, or it can display respect for the child's autonomy. Darling and Steinberg suggested that the effects of any particular technique are influenced by the parenting context in two ways. First, a positive context—for example, one characterized by respect and openness and support for autonomy— may render the child more open to communication with the parent. Second, such a context may make the techniques more effective.

I suggest that a supportive context facilitates needs for relatedness and thus increases the likelihood that a child will internalize regulations. Ryan, Stiller, and Lynch (1994) showed, with a sample of junior high and high school students, that the quality of relatedness to parents and teachers was associated with greater internalization of school behavior. Furthermore, children's feelings of relatedness were a function of how involved and autonomy supportive they felt parents and teachers were. Low relatedness was evident when children described uninvolved and controlling parents; when autonomy support and involvement were present, the children felt high relatedness.

Recent research linking attachment to problems in self-regulation also supports this issue. Children with warm, contingent relations in early life were more likely to comply with parental controls and directives during toddler and preschool years (Sroufe & Fleeson, 1986). Cohn (1990) demonstrated that children with insecure attachments were more aggressive toward peers than those with secure attachments, and Greenberg, Kuschl, and Speltz (1991) observed more insecure attachments in children with oppositional disorders relative to a control group. Richters and Waters (1991) suggested that a positive relationship between parent and child affects the child's readiness for socialization. All of these studies suggest that the effectiveness of parenting techniques depends on the backdrop of relatedness and respect for autonomy provided in the home.

TAKING INTO ACCOUNT THE WAY
THE TECHNIQUE IS DELIVERED

I argued earlier than an autonomy supportive context facilitated intrinsic motivation. I suggest further that the same technique can have a functional significance of control or autonomy support depending on the way it is introduced, expressed, or experienced. For example, the way a limit is set or the tone of a parent's voice in reasoning with a child may determine how the child experiences that particular technique and thus change its effect. Thus, researchers may miss this aspect if they focus on a particular technique without attending to issues such as the locution used, whether feelings about the child's behavior are acknowledged, and so forth. For example, external rewards do not always undermine intrinsic motivation. They do so only when they negate or come into conflict with experiences of autonomy or self-determination (Ryan, Mims, & Koestner, 1983). As I discuss in the next chapter, there are many instances in which rewards may increase intrinsic motivation insofar as they are offered and interpreted as positive feedback regarding one's competence or effectiveness at a task (Deci & Ryan, 1985b; Harackiewicz, Manderlink, & Sansone, 1984; Ryan et al., 1983).

CONCLUSIONS

I have argued that the effects of parental control are not as controversial as one might think, once one has worked through various conceptualizations and definitions. If control is conceived as being "in control"—that is, exercising authority as a parent, maintaining high standards, and confronting and holding children accountable for misbehavior—then there is strong evidence that this type of control is beneficial to children.

On the other hand, I have argued that when control refers to pressuring, intrusive behavior, and motivating children through bribes and other external inducements, then control undermines children's motivation to achieve. It also harms children's sense of themselves as competent and in control and undermines the parent–child relationship. Furthermore, controlling communications undermine children's motivation and adjustment not because they are particular techniques of parenting that don't work but because they conflict with fundamental needs for autonomy inherent in all of us. We simply do not do well (or feel well) when we are made to feel like pawns to others, whether at work, at school, or in our personal relationships. The outcome of such feelings is likely to be one of passive compliance—or perhaps acting in a manner that is opposed to what others would want of us. In either case, if the goal of a parent is to assist in the development of a self-reliant, competent individual, then there are many ways in which control, although well meant, backfires.

The ways we control can be subtle and can be laden with good intentions. Think of a small boy holding a bunch of tulips. To keep the flowers together, he grasps them tightly. By the time he arrives at his grandmother's, the stems are crushed. But he meant well. The same sort of thing can happen to parents who hold on too tightly to their children.

Now let us examine the short- and long-term consequences of controlling styles of parenting—as well as when and how the control backfires.

❧ 4 ❧

Overt and Covert Control

When Anna was 8, her grandmother pulled her aside, looked her in the eyes, and said: "Now you be a good girl to your parents." Anna felt her face go red. What was wrong? Wasn't she being good? After all, people were constantly saying to her: "You're such a good girl." Anna's parents were both blind, and as a result she had extra responsibilities as a child. She also felt like she was constantly being scrutinized.

Sometimes she liked to hide around the house. She would stay extra quiet so that her mother wouldn't find her. But she felt guilty about that because for those moments she wasn't being "a good girl." When she grew up, she felt that "being good" was such an elusive quality. How could she ever be good enough? How could she ever do enough for her parents? Everyone expected so much from her. The praise adults had heaped on her weighed heavily on her psyche and her soul.

I have argued that controlling parenting undermines children's intrinsic motivation and self-confidence and that it results in lower levels of adjustment. I now turn to a more in-depth discussion of behaviors that may be experienced as controlling versus autonomy supportive. Some of the approaches that are obviously controlling are included in this analysis. However, there are others that are far more subtle in their ability to control—notably, rewards and praise. In looking at rewards and praise we can see how the same technique can be administered in a way that either undermines or facilitates a child's self-determination and feelings of competence. Thus, an examination of any technique necessitates attention to the locution with which it is administered, the tone of the interaction, and the context in which it is administered.

CORPORAL PUNISHMENT

"If you don't stop that, I'm going to slap your face."
"Do you want a spanking?"
"This is for your own good."

These are familiar words from our own childhoods, perhaps—but were our parents right when they said that sometimes corporal punishment is necessary? Do children *need* this form of control? Is it beneficial? The answers to these questions may surprise you.

Just what is corporal punishment? Murray Straus, who has spent the last 20 years studying family violence, defined corporal punishment as "the use of physical force with intention of causing a child to experience pain, but not injury, for the purpose of correction or control of the child's behavior" (Straus, 1994, p. 4). With this description Straus attempted to differentiate between corporal punishment, which involves intentional pain infliction without injury, and abuse, in which a child sustains an injury. This line between corporal punishment and abuse is obviously sometimes tricky, as we will soon see.

The most frequent forms of corporal punishment are spanking; slapping; grabbing; shoving a child roughly; or hitting a child with an object such as a hairbrush, belt or paddle. In his work, Straus excluded hitting with objects, because that is more likely to fall into the category of abuse.

The prevalence of physical punishment as a method of discipline is so widespread that it is almost universal. Straus (1994) reported that 90% of parents of toddlers hit their children, and most of these parents continue to do so years later (although the frequency and intensity with which these parents use corporal punishment clearly vary tremendously). Corporal punishment is legal in every state in the United States.

Many studies regarding the use of corporal punishment have been conducted from a sociological point of view in that they focus on who uses spanking and what the ramifications are for violence in our society. What is lacking is a psychological perspective. I have found Hoffman's work on power assertive techniques useful for understanding the meaning of physical punishment to children. The purposeful use of physical punishment is the prototype of what Hoffman (1970) considers a power assertive technique. Hoffman differentiates between techniques that assert power or apply external pressure and those that attempt to gain voluntary behavior change by inducing internal change in the child. Physical punishment is literally the most coercive among the power assertive techniques—which also include threats, direct commands, and deprivations—because it relies on the parent's power, including the adult's physical size, as well as the child's fear.

According to Straus (1994), there are a number of reasons why corporal punishment is not a good idea—aside from the fact that it is prototypically controlling and, from a self-determination perspective, unlikely to facilitate change in the child. First, it legitimizes other forms of violence. It gives the message that if something goes wrong and other methods of stopping it do not work, it is all right to use physical violence. This is certainly not a message that most parents wish to convey to their children. A second reason is the fact that corporal punishment has a high risk of escalating into abuse. Most cases of physical abuse begin with corporal punishment, then spiral out of control (Kadushin & Martin, 1981). Because much hitting occurs when a parent is angry and out of control (Carson, 1988), the use of any form of corporal punishment creates a risky situation.

A third reason is humane. As Straus (1994) pointed out in his compelling book *Beating the Devil Out of Them*, in the United States it is no longer permissible to hit servants, apprentices, wives, prisoners, and members of the armed forces. It is curious that the hitting of children is still allowed and that children's rights are considered different from those of other groups. In a humane society there would, one would presume, be protection against all physical assault.

From a self-determination perspective, physical forms of discipline are prototypically controlling. They pressure the child to behave in specific ways by using fear of pain and humiliation, and they undermine a sense of choice or autonomy. Furthermore, they undermine the sense of relatedness in that it is inherently contradictory and confusing that a person who loves you inflicts pain. When parents physically punish their children, the children begin avoiding parents because they fear them. This obviously interferes with a child's feeling of security and relatedness (Maccoby, 1980).

Putting theoretical notions and psychological perspectives aside, however, what are the empirical data regarding physical punishment as a disciplinary technique? Is there evidence that it is detrimental to children's development? In some ways, the answer to this question depends on the literature one reads; the use of spanking has become a heated debate in the psychological community. Some researchers, including Straus, have lined up on the anti-spanking side, whereas others (e.g., Baumrind, 1996; Larzelere, 2000) have suggested that the evidence does not support a wholesale ban on spanking. The stakes in this debate are high in that Canada is considering banning corporal punishment and Sweden and Norway have already done so.

In their classic study, Sears, Maccoby, and Levin (1957) found that children of parents who used physical methods of punishment were more aggressive than other children. Strassberg, Dodge, Petit, and Bates (1994) found that parents of elementary school children who were spanked had double the rate of physical aggression against other children in school. On the basis of the National Family Violence Survey, Straus (1983) found that children who were spanked frequently were four times more likely to repeatedly hit a sibling than children who were not spanked.

These studies might compel a parent to avoid physical punishment, but they, like many others, suffer from a methodological problem: They fail to control for earlier levels of misbehavior. As Larzelere, Kuhn, and Johnson (2000) described as the problem of "intervention selection bias," every disciplinary tactic, including reasoning and explaining, is associated with misbehavior in the child because it is the misbehavior that elicits the disciplinary steps taken by the parent. In other words, physical punishment may be associated with child aggression because it causes it or because more aggressive children are more likely to be physically punished by their parents. Thus, studies must account for earlier misbehavior if they are to address the effects of physical punishment.

To improve on the correlational findings in the literature, Straus, Sugarman, and Giles-Sims (1997) used a longitudinal design and showed that, controlling for level of antisocial behavior in children at the start of the study, as well as socioeconomic status, sex of child, and the extent to which the home provided emotional support and cognitive stimulation, the higher the levels of spanking at the start of the 2-year period, the higher the level of antisocial behavior 2 years later. However, Larzelere (2000) took issue with this and other Straus studies, suggesting that Straus did not adequately control for prior child misbehavior. To evaluate the research, Larzelere reviewed 38 studies of physical punishment conducted between 1995 and 2000. Excluding studies of what he termed *abusive* punishment, he found that 32% of studies showed a beneficial effect, 34% showed a detrimental effect, and 34% showed a mixed effect. Quite pertinent to the present discussion is that when there was a beneficial effect, it was mostly short term (directly after the behavior). Furthermore, the outcome examined was most likely to be compliance. Thus, a child who persists in hitting his sibling and is spanked usually stops. More problematic, however, are the long-term effects of spanking as well as the side effects for the parent–child relationship. Although spanking may stop aggressive behavior right after the incident, there is no assurance of long-term compliance and some evidence that it may interfere with such long-term effects.

The debate goes on. Although there is much disagreement about the message the literature sends, researchers do agree about a few things. First, intense and frequent physical punishment is detrimental to children. Second, physical punishment should never be the first choice as a disciplinary technique. Larzelere, Sather, Schneider, Larson, and Pike (1998), for example, suggest that parents would be wise to try other tactics first and resort to spanking only when the other tactics do not work. A third point of agreement is that parents should never strike children out of anger or loss of control. Spanking should be a reasoned decision parents make as part of their repertoire of disciplinary techniques.

My own reading of the literature leads me to several conclusions. First, there is no evidence that physical punishment is beneficial to children's self-regulation and some that it is detrimental. Furthermore, it is quite risky to assume that the physical punishment will not get out of control. As stated earlier, most episodes of abuse begin with a disciplinary spanking. Thus, to suggest that physical punishment and abusive punishment can be completely separated seems naïve at best. Finally, because there are other choices that are more likely to facilitate internalization without the risk of negative side effects, it is prudent to avoid physical punishment.

In talking to parents, I am often struck by the fact that they do not want to use physical punishment. They tell me that they reserve it for the most important child challenges—those in which the stakes are the highest, such as safety. When it comes to lying, these parents would not hit. However, when it comes to crossing the street without looking, they say physical punishment is more justified.

There is no reason to believe that physical methods are more effective in these situations than in others. It is true that we, as parents, want to reserve our most effective strategies for the most crucial situations. However, we should not think that a strategy is effective just because it uses the biggest guns. Key times call for more of what we know works—not less. And we know that clear consequences; explanations; time; and deliberate, rather than impulsive, strategies, work.

REWARDS

When our eldest daughter was about 2½, my husband and I began potty training her. She displayed little interest in using the toilet and, despite my explanations about the benefits of giving up diapers, she made it clear that she was not giving them up without a battle. She was going to start a preschool in the fall that wouldn't accept her if she were still in diapers. I became afraid of the consequences, so I developed a star chart. (A discussion of how parents fall into traps like these follows in a later chapter.)

Each time my daughter used the potty, she received a star. When a line of stars was filled in, she would be able to choose an activity that we would do together.

The first day, everything went fine.

The second day, the allure of the stars' promise faded. She became much more interested in seeing my reaction when she refused the potty. By upping the ante, I had created a more fascinating and greater challenge for her.

I saw the error of my ways. I gave up the star chart, sat her down, and said, "When you are ready to give up diapers and use the potty, you let me know." The next day she used the potty and was never in diapers again. I realize this story sounds extreme. But it is true.

Rewards, because they are positive and desired, are an insidious form of control. The use of rewards or contingency programs is widespread in educational and home settings. Such programs are particularly popular with special populations such as children enrolled in special education programs and developmentally disabled and mentally ill individuals. Parenting experts advocate the use of rewards such as star charts, tokens for a job well done, or monetary rewards for good behavior or performance. How can such positive methods be detrimental?

The first experimental studies of intrinsic motivation actually focused on rewards. In Deci's (1971) initial studies, college students were given fun tasks in the form of Soma puzzles to complete. Half the students were told they would receive money for doing the puzzles. The other half were not. They set to work. At the end of a predetermined period of time, the experimenter stopped the puzzlers and announced the experiment was over. Saying he had to leave the room for a few moments, the experimenter casually mentioned that the students could pass the time by doing more of the puzzles or by reading some magazines. He then surreptitiously observed the students to see what they would do. This interval was the free-choice period, because there were no pressures or incentives to do the task.

The findings were striking: The students who were rewarded spent less time on the puzzles when given a choice. How do we explain this? The students who were rewarded presumably no longer felt they were doing the activity for fun. They now were doing the activity for the reward. They no longer felt autonomous. When given the opportunity to choose to do puzzles or not—without rewards—the students chose to do other things. Thus, although rewards may increase motivation while they are in effect, after they are withdrawn, motivation decreases—and the level of decrease is striking. Motivation drops not to the level it was before the rewards but *below* that of the initial motivation. In other words, rewards have neither a positive nor a neutral effect. Rewards undermine intrinsic motivation.[1]

---

[1]Whether rewards undermine intrinsic motivation is a point of controversy. From a behaviorist standpoint, while rewards are in effect they should increase the rate of behavior. However, when rewards are no longer in effect, behavior should revert to its original rate (the baseline). Intrinsic motivation theory, by contrast, suggests that after the imposition of rewards, engagement in the activity will fall to a level below the baseline (the undermining effect). Behavioral theorists have used a number of arguments to refute the undermining effect. Some, for example, have stated that they have conducted similar experiments and have not replicated the undermining effect (e.g., Feingold & Mahoney, 1975). Others have suggested that doing an activity under a reward condition simply (continued on next page)

Is the negative effect of rewards on intrinsic motivation relevant to children? Lepper and Greene (1975) conducted the first experiment to show that it is. They asked 3- and 4-year-olds to work with attractive Magic Markers and construction paper, an activity that children of this age find enjoyable. Children in one group were told they would receive a Good Player Award if they did some drawings for the experimenter. The award, to be placed on a bulletin board, contained the child's name, a gold star, and a red ribbon. For the second group, there was no mention of an award. Several days later, children were again brought to the laboratory. They were given a choice to work with the same Magic Markers or to do something else. Children who had gotten the Good Player Award spent significantly less time playing with the art materials than those who had not gotten the award.

These results may seem somewhat contradictory. Children love to get stickers and other rewards. We may think rewarding them for doing the things they enjoy will only give them more reason to do those things. However, as Richard deCharms (1968) noted, when children do activities for the reward rather than the joy of the activity, they no longer get the feelings of freedom, competence, and pleasure that they had gotten. Their play has turned into work.

Rewards, as I have illustrated, provide an external reason for engaging in an activity, thereby changing one's locus of causality for the activity from internal to external. Rewards are external stimuli that channel people's behavior and thus take away their sense of freedom and choice.

However, rewards are used extensively, particularly in the academic domain. Do parents believe that rewards will enhance motivation? One set of studies suggests that the answer to this question is yes and that the negative effects of rewards are counterintuitive. Boggiano, Barrett, Weiher, McClelland, and Lusk (1987) presented parents with a number of scenarios involving children. These included a scenario in which a child showed a high degree of academic interest and one in which a child showed a low degree of academic interest, as well as scenarios involving aggression and altruistic behavior. They then asked parents to choose from among the following strategies to increase motivation: reward, reasoning, punishment, or not interfering. For the academic domain, parents preferred rewards, whereas for the other domains this was not the case. Furthermore, they preferred to use rewards whether the child was showing high or low academic interest and regardless of whether they were trying to induce short- or long-term changes in the children. Boggiano et al. (1987) showed that parents

(*continued from previous page*)   distracts the individual (e.g., Reiss & Sushinsky, 1975) and that this accounts for the undermining effect. For a discussion of these critiques, interested readers are referred to Eisenberger and Cameron's (1996) article and Cameron and Pierce's (1994) article. For a refutation of various critiques, readers should see Deci and Ryan's (1985b) book or Deci, Koestner, and Ryan's (1999) article.

adhered to the following principle: The bigger the reward, the higher the motivation.

Why would the negative effects of rewards be especially counterintuitive in the academic domain? First, Boggiano et al. (1987) argued, performance in school is so often paired with reward that parents are accustomed to this state of affairs. In U.S. schools grades are emphasized, rewards are given out for memorizing multiplication tables, and children receive prizes for reading a particular number of books. Because school personnel engage in the use of rewards so frequently, parents then assume it is the appropriate and helpful thing to do. Furthermore, parents typically use such techniques in low-interest situations—such as when a child is not doing his or her homework. They may indeed see some increases in on-task behavior, at least in the short term and for activities the child does not enjoy. Parents then generalize from the low-interest, short-term situation to all academic situations. Parents begin using rewards in situations in which the child might otherwise enjoy the activity, thus undermining any intrinsic motivation that might have been there.

Is it ever useful to use rewards with children? Rewards can be useful in low-interest or boring activities, such as taking out the garbage (if it is not a regular chore assigned as part of household responsibilities) or memorizing spelling words. The reward provides a reason for a child to engage in an activity that he or she would not otherwise pursue. The reward may increase the likelihood that the child will do what the parent wants—at least while the reward is in effect. However, because rewards induce an external locus of causality they undermine the possibility of the child moving to a point of being able to value the activity more. Even extrinsically motivated activities can be more or less autonomously regulated, and parents' goals may be to facilitate as much as autonomy as possible. Thus, the goals of enhancing natural interests as well as facilitating greater autonomy for nonintrinsically motivated activity are both undermined by reliance on rewards.

DIFFERENT TYPES OF REWARDS

Although I have argued that rewards undermine intrinsic motivation, the type of reward that parents administer can make a difference, and parents can use rewards in ways that make positive effects most likely. For example, rewards will be most undermining of children's intrinsic motivation when they are salient and expected rather than unexpected. Ross (1975) rewarded two sets of students for engaging in an interesting activity. Half of the participants were reminded about the reward, and the other half were not. The results revealed a reduction for the salient-reward group but not for the no-cue group. Lepper, Greene, and Nisbett

(1973) told preschoolers in one group before they began an activity that they would receive a reward for doing the activity, whereas those in a second group received unexpected rewards after they had completed an activity. Compared to the no-reward group, the expected-reward group showed significant declines in intrinsic motivation, whereas the unexpected-reward group did not.

Thus, the more frequently parents use rewards and remind children that the children are doing activities for the reward, the more they undermine children's sense of autonomy for the activity. If a parent does use rewards, the most adaptive way is to give them unexpectedly. For example, a good report card may elicit such joy in a parent that he or she may suggest the whole family go out to dinner to celebrate. How different this is than stressing to the child that the reason to get good grades is so that the family can go out to dinner. The unexpected reward emphasizes to the child his or her competence, whereas the expected reward makes the task a means to an end. Readers might recall teachers they had as children who told them that the reason to study was because they would be graded. Emphasizing the grade is a way to make the reward salient and induce an external locus of causality for the behavior, thereby undermining any internal reason to pursue the material.

A final issue is one that I pursue further in the next section: the degree to which the reward signifies competence or control. Rewards can be administered in different ways, and these ways have different consequences (Ryan et al., 1983). You can give someone a reward for doing an activity—say, writing a story. First, the reward can be given for coming to the storytelling session. Such a reward is task noncontingent in that the person does not have to do anything in particular in the session to obtain the reward. He or she just needs to show up. On the other hand, you can give someone a reward for writing the story. In this case, the reward is task contingent. Finally, you can give someone a reward depending upon how well the story is written. Such a reward is performance contingent because its administration depends on the quality of the outcome.

Ryan et al. (1983) compared the effects of these different types of rewards on intrinsic motivation. They found that task-contingent rewards were the most undermining of motivation and that performance-contingent rewards the least. Why would this be? One reason is that rewards can carry two types of information: a controlling aspect, which induces the person to behave because of the reward, and a feedback aspect, which conveys information about one's competence. Because the performance-contingent reward not only controls but also conveys positive feedback—meaning that receiving the reward signifies that one did a good job—it may have an enhancing component. Obtaining the reward means that one did a good job, and competence feedback facilitates intrinsic motivation. On the other hand, the task-contingent reward contains only the controlling contingency without the message that one is doing a good job. However, whether the competence-enhancing or controlling aspect of the reward is more salient depends on how feedback is administered, that is, its interpersonal context. This is the topic of the next section.

PRAISE AND FEEDBACK

Everyone likes to get positive feedback for a job well done and, consistent with this, positive feedback has been shown to enhance intrinsic motivation. From a self-determination viewpoint, positive feedback satisfies the need for competence that underlies intrinsic motivation. When individuals receive positive feedback, they feel more competent, and their intrinsic motivation is enhanced. Deci (1971) showed that participants who received positive verbal feedback from the experimenter for working on puzzles were more intrinsically motivated in a subsequent free-choice period than participants who received no feedback. On the other side, negative feedback undermines intrinsic motivation. For example, in one study (Deci & Cascio, 1972), participants were told, "Although you did solve that one, your time was below average." Such feedback made it less likely that participants would pursue the activity in a subsequent free-choice period.

We simply do not do well when we feel incompetent. So, is more praise better? Should we advocate parents lavishing praise on children? The answer is equivocal, for praise has a dark side. Two aspects of this dark side have been the focus of research: (a) the controlling versus autonomy supportive nature of praise and (b) whether the praise is for global (person) or specific (products) issues.

Research on praise was constrained for some time by the notion that praise is positive reinforcement and that its form makes no difference. However, recent studies have shown that the specific language of praise does make a difference in that it conveys different messages to the person. Before addressing the different ways praise can be administered, I address its definition. *Praise* has been described as "positive evaluation of another's products, performance or attributes where the evaluator presumes the validity of the standards on which the evaluation is based" (Kanouse, Gumpert, & Canavan-Gumpert, 1981, p. 98). Thus, praise is evaluative in nature. Furthermore, different dimensions of praise have been examined. Praise can be specific or general. For example, "You are a good writer" is a general statement, and "Your paragraphs are especially tight," is specific. Praise can also be of the person or of the product or action. Think of "You are an angel" versus "Your behavior was good today."

CONTROLLING VERSUS INFORMATIONAL PRAISE

Just as with any communication, praise can be conveyed in a controlling or an informational manner. Ryan (1982) reasoned that praise that is controlling signifies the praiser's investment in specific behavioral outcomes. Thus, controlling praise signifies that the praiser wants the person to perform to a specified level and is taking an evaluative stance. The praise carries with it an expectation of how the person "should" do, which is experienced as pressure to perform. On the other hand, informational feedback simply provides information on how well one did or the appropriateness of one's behavior, without the pressure to obtain particular standards.

In a study illustrating the different aspects of praise, Ryan (1982) used Al Hirschfeld drawings from *The New York Times*, in which the author hid his daughter's name (NINA) in the pictures. Ryan had his introductory psychology students find these hidden "NINAs," an interesting task for college students. After completing the puzzles, all students received feedback about their performance. This feedback compared their performance with that of the "average" student, who was always a bit below their own average. Thus, all participants got positive feedback. In addition to this feedback, however, one half of the participants also received an evaluative statement after each puzzle. The statements were designed to be controlling in that they signified the experimenter's investment in the participant doing well and pressure to maintain a standard. For example, the participants were told, "Excellent. You should keep up the good work" or "Good. You're doing as well as you should." Participants who received the controlling evaluative statements spent less time on similar puzzles during a free-choice session than those who did not receive this feedback.

Kast and Connor (1988) gave third-, fifth-, and eighth-grade students grids with embedded words to complete. They then gave some children informational feedback, such as "Good. You did very well on this game. You were right on almost all the puzzles," or they provided controlling feedback: "Good. Keep it up. I would like you to do even better on the next game." Afterward, they asked children how much they liked the word search game. Children who had received informational feedback reported liking the game more than those who had received controlling praise.

Thus, as parents praise children, the intentions they have and their resulting communications may determine the effect of the praise. Are parents simply giving feedback, or do they have an agenda of "getting more" or manipulating the child into further performance when they administer it? How praise is phrased, and whether it is used as a tool to control children's behavior or as feedback without other motives, can make the words enhancing or undermining.

PERSON VERSUS PRODUCT PRAISE

Praise may be directed at a person or at the person's products, actions, or the consequences of his or her actions. Dweck and her colleagues (e.g., Kamins &

Dweck, 1999; Mueller & Dweck, 1998), for example, recently examined the effects of feedback directed at the child as a whole versus feedback directed at the child's effort. Although it may be intuitive that criticizing the child (e.g., "You're bad!") instead of focusing on his or her behavior (e.g., "I don't like what you are doing") is bound to have negative effects, the problematic effects of person praise may be less obvious. Many years ago, Ginott (1965) cautioned against the use of praise with children. When you tell your child that he is an angel, he invariably reacts with "devilish" behavior. Why?

The answer is that praise focused on the child implies that future performance will need to meet the praiser's standards. Thus, it is perceived as controlling. Farson (1963) wrote convincingly that

> the most threatening aspect of praise is the obligation it puts on us to be praiseworthy people.... For if we really believe it when we are told that we are competent, or intelligent, or beautiful, then we are continually on the spot to be competent, or intelligent, or beautiful, not only in the eyes of the person who praised us, but, even worse, in our own eyes. (p. 63)

When a parent praises a child for doing well (e.g., "You're a good girl/boy,") he or she is teaching the child that competence or self-worth is contingent on performance. The child then feels pressure to perform in a way that makes him or her appear "good." This may have especially problematic sequelae when the child encounters difficulties.

Kamins and Dweck (1999) illustrated this issue in a study in which kindergarten children were told a story in which they were asked to imagine that they had completed a puzzle successfully. The teacher in the story then administered either person praise ("I'm very proud of you," or "You're a good girl," or, "You're really good at this") or outcome or process praise ("That's the right way to do it," or "You must have tried really hard"). The children in both groups were equivalent in their desire to do more puzzles, in their affect, and in their ratings of their imagined performance. However, then they were given two scenarios in which they imagined that they had made a mistake. At that point, children in the person praise group rated themselves as less good at the task. They also rated their products as less positive, and they were less interested than the children who had received process praise in doing further tasks. Person praise is controlling in that it pressures children to "perform" and focuses them on themselves rather than on the task at hand, thus undermining their intrinsic motivation to pursue tasks for their own sake.

I now turn to another issue involving praise. Mueller and Dweck (1998) reasoned that a particular kind of person praise—that for intelligence—would be perceived by children as pressure to continue to "look smart" and, as such, would undermine their tendencies to focus on increasing their knowledge in learning activities. In their studies, Mueller and Dweck (1998) had children complete a series of matrices. After they completed the task, the children were told "Wow, you did very well on these problems. You got *x number* right. That's a really high score." Then half of the children were told "You must be smart at these problems," and the other half were told "You must have worked hard at these problems." Children were then given another set of problems on which they did not do as well. They were then asked how much they enjoyed these problems and whether they would like to do either some more "problems that aren't too hard so I don't get many wrong," or problems that "I'll learn a lot from even if I won't look so smart." Children who had been praised for their intelligence tended to say that they did not enjoy doing the problems and tended to choose easy problems that made them look good. They also were more likely to say that the reason they failed when they did not do well was because they did not have the ability. Children who had been praised for the effort they had made tended to enjoy the problems to a greater degree and they picked more difficult problems that would teach them more.

According to Mueller and Dweck (1998), praise for intelligence focuses children on the goal of doing well and looking good—a performance goal—rather than a goal of learning the material. This pressure to continue to be smart presumably undermines the goal of learning and mastering material that entails the risk of doing poorly.

Again, this is a counterintuitive finding. In a recent survey of parents, 85% believed that praising their children's ability would help their children (Mueller & Dweck, 1996), endorsing the statement "it is necessary to praise children's ability when they perform well on a task to make them feel that they are smart." Such a viewpoint may be fueled by the fact that parents see the positive effects of praise for intelligence when their children are succeeding. However, it is when things get tough and children experience failure that we see the negative effects of the kind of praise that focuses children on performance and not learning. This is when praise goes awry.

LOVE WITHDRAWAL
AND CONDITIONAL PARENTAL REGARD

When my younger daughter reached second grade, she was assigned school projects to do at home. One day, she was preparing a presentation on the American Society for the Prevention of Cruelty to Animals and asked me to help. She began her writing with a detail that obviously could not be at the beginning. My several attempts at gentle assistance were met with anger on her part. "This is my project!" she said. "IT'S FINE!" she told me at another point.

At my wits' end—for I had not made dinner yet and had literally 12 phone calls to return—I yelled: "Okay, do it yourself. I'm not helping you anymore," and stormed out of the room. What came next was a desperate plea for my return. She followed me, saying, "I *need* you."

At that moment it struck me how powerful it is to threaten to be unavailable to our children.

Children's need for love, attention, and approval from their parents is a powerful one that lasts across the life span. Techniques that manipulate this need and threaten loss of support are bound to have strong effects on children. One that fits this description is the withdrawal of love. In this technique, parents withdraw their attention or affection when the child does something they do not like. They may refuse to communicate and may physically separate themselves from the child.

It is interesting that the use of such strategies has received less attention from researchers than might be expected. Part of the reason is that, when asked about these techniques, parents report that they use them infrequently. However, parents use withdrawal in conjunction with other techniques, such as physical punishment and explanation or induction. It is also likely that withdrawal is used more often than parents would like to admit.

The power of love withdrawal rests on children's dependence and fear of abandonment. Because children are so dependent on parents, the threat of withdrawal of attention and love arouses strong feelings of fear and anxiety and perhaps even shame and guilt (Potter-Efron, 1989). These feelings then motivate children to behave. Thus, rather than being pushed from without by strong incentives, such as rewards or punishments, the child experiences negative feelings that motivate the child to push him- or herself. This internal pressure, or *compulsion*, is antithetical to a feeling of autonomy, because the child cannot choose to risk noncompliance—the stakes are simply too high. Thus, parents' use of love withdrawal is perceived as a controlling technique, albeit one that would lead the child to push or pressure himself internally rather than feel external pressure to avoid negative feelings and fears. Despite the fact that the control is internal, it can be as aversive and powerful as any push from without.

The little research that has examined love withdrawal has, unsurprisingly, shown negative findings. Coopersmith (1967) showed that mothers of boys with low self-esteem tended to be high in the use of love withdrawal. Chapman and Zahn-Waxler (1982), in a study of moral development that I discuss further in Chapter 5 showed that high use of love withdrawal was related to short- but not long-term compliance and that children were more likely to avoid their caretakers later. Chapman and Zahn-Waxler further argued that this technique is antithetical to a prosocial or empathic orientation because it focuses the child on his or her own emotions rather than on the emotions of the other person.

Assor, Roth, and Deci (1999) examined a related phenomenon: parents' conditioning of their regard on specific attributes of their children. In a series of studies, they asked college students whether, in their childhoods, their parents had shown their affection and love conditionally—based on the child displaying some attribute or performance. Specifically, Assor et al. asked whether parents showed affection, esteem, or attention dependent on their performance in four domains: academics, sports, prosocial behavior, and control of negative emotions. For example, one item read "As a child, I often felt that my mother/father would give me more affection than usual if I did well in sports." The authors presumed that conditioning of love would be perceived as a coercive attempt to control children and would thus be associated with feelings of being controlled in childhood and with anger toward parents. They also reasoned that, if children did engage in the activity—for example, sports—under such conditions they would do so not because they felt a sense of choice or desire but because they felt they "had to" or because of an internal compulsion. As expected, the findings revealed that students who reported more conditional regard in childhood felt more controlled and reported more anger at their parents. A path analysis supported the model that when children did engage in an activity under conditions in which parental regard was tied to performance, they did so out of a sense of compulsion rather than of choice. These results support the idea that conditional love is clearly perceived as controlling. Although often subtle, its effects can be quite harmful.

ADDENDUM:
TECHNIQUES THAT ARE AUTONOMY SUPPORTIVE

Throughout my discussion of overt and covert controlling techniques, I have contrasted such techniques with other possibilities. I have discussed controlling versus noncontrolling feedback, controlling and noncontrolling praise, and the use of rewards versus noncontrolling limit setting. In this section I more explicitly describe some other techniques that I have not yet contrasted with control that might be considered autonomy supportive. I reiterate here, however, that the effect of any technique depends on the style in which it is administered.

One technique that has been found in experimental studies to facilitate intrinsic motivation is the introduction of choice. The feeling of choicefulness is a hallmark of autonomy, and thus providing choice would be highly autonomy supportive. Zuckerman, Porac, Lathin, Smith, and Deci (1978), for example, had college students work on interesting puzzles. Half of the students were allowed to make choices about the task, and half were assigned the choices that the other group made. Participants who were given a choice were more intrinsically motivated to pursue the puzzles later than those who were given no choice. This effect was replicated with children in a study conducted by Swann and Pittman (1977).

Another technique that would be highly autonomy supportive is acknowledging the individual's feelings about engaging in an activity. For example, Koestner et al. (1984) set limits on young children's painting activities in two ways: They either acknowledged that the children did not wish to comply with the limits, or they did not provide this acknowledgment. When children's feelings were acknowledged, they were later more intrinsically motivated and showed more positive affect toward painting than children whose feelings had not been acknowledged. Thus, when limits need to be set, acknowledging that children may not always wish to follow them decreases the pressure and control children experience.

Lepper and his colleagues have explored the use of fantasy techniques to facilitate children's motivation and learning. They have reasoned that when tasks are presented in ways that capitalize on children's interests, children will become more involved with them. L. Parker and Lepper (1992) taught children a graphics program in one of two conditions. In the first condition, the program was presented in abstract form—children were to navigate around the computer in specified ways. In the second condition, a fantasy condition, the computer display had been embellished to look like islands, and the task was to search for buried treasure. Children who used the fantasy programs found them to be more fun and interesting than those exposed to the nonembellished forms. They also showed greater subsequent learning. In a study with a similar design, Cordova and Lepper (1996) had children work on computer programs in fantasy or no-fantasy conditions. Furthermore, some of the children had a choice about what kind of information was included in the fantasy, and some did not. Children whose learning involved interesting fantasy materials—and, in particular, children who had a choice in the materials—were more engaged in the task, learned more, and were more likely to say that they would stay after school or during recess to play with the computer programs than did children in the no-fantasy condition.

The techniques just discussed—choice, acknowledgment of feelings, and increasing the interest value of activities—are just some of the possible techniques parents can use to facilitate children's motivation and engagement. Such techniques not only facilitate engagement in activities but also create the positive context that will make disciplinary techniques more likely to be effective and thus minimize the need for further control. Because they support children's autonomy, they are also more likely to facilitate children's engagement in an activity for internalized reasons rather than because they fear parental consequences. The ways in which parent styles facilitate and undermine children's taking on the regulation of their own behavior is the topic of chapter 5.

CONCLUSIONS

What does this review of various parenting techniques say about control? Control can certainly be overt, as in the use of physically coercive punishments. The effects of overt control are indisputably negative. However, control can be disguised as positive, as in the use of rewards and praise, which, although desired, can undermine a child's sense of choice and interest. Perhaps most insidious is the use of love-oriented techniques that hinge parents' love and affection on a child's behavior. Not only will these methods result in less autonomous behavior, but underlying them is a message of deficiency, that the child will never be good enough or lovable enough. These techniques are bound to have long-term effects on children's feelings about themselves and about their abilities.

5

Differentiating the Effects of Control: Compliance Versus Internalization

Although most adults assume that fairy tales were constructed as morality lessons or fear reducers for children, there is one type that can actually serve as a tale for adults. Think of the many stories from the Brothers Grimm that center on highly controlling parents or stepparents. Inevitably in these stories the children rebel. The Worn-Out Dancing Shoes is an excellent example. Each night a king locks up his 12 daughters. He cannot understand why their dancing shoes are in tatters the next morning, but he cannot ask them outright what the matter is. There is no relationship between the king and his daughters. Instead, he has to send princes to spy on his daughters to find out what they are doing. There is no question of the king and his daughters talking face to face.

It is not particularly challenging for parents to get their children to do things. In typical instances in which parents try to change children's behavior, the parents are successful over 75% of the time (Hoffman, 1960; Minton, Kagan, & Levine, 1971). If mother wants to get her child to clean his or her room, she need only offer a big enough incentive—say, $10, or a new bicycle. A highly salient and aversive threat of punishment—perhaps the threat of foregoing a birthday party—might also do the trick. Obtaining compliance can certainly be achieved by force from without.

More challenging, however, is to create the kind of change that involves not just outward compliance but also an inner endorsement and valuing of the ac-

51

tivity. More than compliance per se, the goals of parents are often to have their children take on the responsibility for their own behavior and value the activity themselves. Parents do not want to have to offer a reward for room cleaning, for example, but prefer that children initiate and follow through on their own. Parents may want their children to *want* to clean their rooms, to help someone else because children think it is the right thing to do—rather than because they will get in trouble for not doing it—or to behave according to societal standards when no one is looking. After all, one of the goals of socialization is to have a child who is not simply compliant but one who embodies values consistent with the culture and family. As I have discussed, facilitating interest as well as curious and creative behavior is also desirable, as is creating a strong and intimate parent–child relationship.

In this chapter I provide a perspective from which to understand how children move from an external stance to an internalized stance toward activities or behaviors to which they are not naturally or spontaneously predisposed. It is here that control becomes an interesting part of the paradox of socialization. We can force a behavior, but we cannot force a child to "own" the values and attitudes behind the behavior. We can teach the values we hold dear, but we cannot force a child to cherish those same values. According to self-determination theory, taking on social values as their own is something children are naturally oriented to do. It is also something that must be actively achieved by the child. Because of this, parents and other caretakers face the important challenge of how to mobilize, facilitate, and support a child's natural tendency to internalize cultural values, attitudes, and behaviors.

AN ACTIVE MODEL OF SOCIALIZATION

Determining how to facilitate children's adoption of the values and behaviors of their parents and the culture around them entails specifying a model of how children are socialized. Early theories of how children became functioning members of society viewed the socialization process as moving from parent to child (Kuczynski, Harach, & Bernardini, 1999). The child was a receptacle to be filled with a full set of knowledge and behaviors. Children were depicted as passive recipients of this information. Underlying this passive model was the assumption that, within the parent–child interaction, parents were powerful and children powerless. In such a unilateral model of parent–child relationships parents influence their children far more than the reverse.

More recent models of socialization question this passive model and have replaced it with a view of children as active participants in their own development and socialization. Parents and children are seen as causal agents, each influencing each other's behavior and each dependent on the other. Even if the child has less actual power in the relationship (i.e., the parent may have the ultimate say in whether the child can go out at night or whether he or she is allowed to play football), this should not be equated with a passive child or with unidirectional causality. Even in their struggles and resistance, children are actively influencing their parents. Such a bilateral model of parent–child relations (Lollis & Kuczynski, 1997) is consistent with research I review in chapter 7 showing how children actively shape their parents' reactions and behavior.

Self-determination theory is one theory that can be characterized as depicting an active, agentic child. As I suggested earlier, self-determination theory begins with the idea that humans are born with innate propensities to be active and agentic with regard to their surroundings. Individuals are born with the energy to pursue challenges and master their environment. Self-determination theory is an organismic theory because it assumes that humans engage their surroundings in an attempt to elaborate and expand themselves and thus to grow and develop. This innate developmental process is called *organismic integration*.

One corollary of the assumption that individuals are naturally inclined to elaborate themselves over the life span is that they have a readiness to absorb and accept socially transmitted values and practices as they develop a more complex and unified self (Ryan, 1995). However, consistent with this view, children don't just accept parental behaviors and beliefs as such; they actively make sense of parental messages, finding meaning in them. Furthermore, as they accept these messages they transform them and actively integrate them. The process of accepting values and behaviors by actively transforming them into personal values and autonomously self-regulated behavior is called *internalization* (Kelman, 1961; Meissner, 1981; Schafer, 1968). Although the concept of internalization has been criticized as being a unilateral imprinting of the parent's views on the child (Kuczynski et al., 1999), in self-determination theory internalization is conceptualized as an active developmental process in which children, as well as adolescents and adults, progressively transform and integrate societal values and proscriptions into a coherent sense of self.

WHEN IS INTERNALIZATION RELEVANT?

Earlier I discussed intrinsic motivation, the energy source that fuels spontaneously interesting activities—say, play, exploration, and solving interesting problems. Adults do not have to prod children to engage in these activities. They do so willingly and without prompts. The motivation to engage in these behaviors is not separate from the activity itself. Instead, the motivation stems from the inherent enjoyment and feelings of freedom and competence people experience as they engage in their chosen pursuit. We saw earlier how controls can undermine children's intrinsic motivation to pursue activities, thereby turning play into work.

However, many behaviors that adults want children to pursue are not intrinsically motivated. Children may not spontaneously pursue learning their multiplication tables, going to bed on time, or sharing their toys. Children do these activities not for their inherent interest or enjoyment but for some reward or desired consequence that is separate from the activity itself. We refer to these activities as *extrinsically motivated*. Their motivation is separate from, or extrinsic to, the activity. Extrinsic motivation thus refers to any behavior that is pursued for some instrumental goal or consequence ("in order to ..."), whether that consequence is administered interpersonally (from without) or intrapsychically (from within the person). Extrinsic motivation subsumes instances in which children behave as a direct function of rules, demands, threats, or proffered rewards as well as instances in which children behave to maintain a fragile sense of self-esteem or simply because they think it is important for their health or well-being. All of these goals are separate from the activity itself.

As just characterized, extrinsic motives can be highly varied. Some stem from the person; others from external sources. Some involve a sense of choicefulness; others a feeling of being compelled. A critical dimension on which extrinsic motives vary is the extent to which they are self-determined versus regulated by externally imposed constraints, rewards, or punishments (Ryan, Connell, & Deci, 1985).

INTERNALIZATION DEFINED

Internalization is the process through which individuals acquire beliefs, attitudes, and behavioral regulations from external sources and progressively transform those external regulations into personal attributes, values, or regulatory styles. This process is further presumed to be not an all-or-none phenomenon but a question of degrees. Ryan and Connell (1989) proposed a continuum of internalization to describe how fully a value or regulation has been "taken in" and integrated into the person's value system or sense of self. The four types of self-regulation that lie along this continuum are depicted in Figure 5.1.

At the least self-determined end of the spectrum, behaviors in the extrinsic domain are motivated by external contingencies such as demands, requests, rewards, and punishments administered by caretakers. In this instance, the behavior would not be undertaken if these demands were not present. For example, a child who cleans her room because she would get yelled at or punished if she didn't displays *external regulation* of her behavior. The child at this

TYPES OF SELF-REGULATION

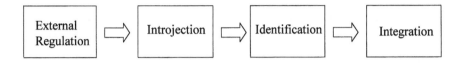

FIG. 5.1.   Types of self-regulation.

level does not feel as if she has choice but rather feels controlled and coerced. A greater degree of internalization is seen in *introjected regulation*. Here, externally imposed regulations have been "taken in" by the person but are maintained in essentially their original form. The result is that the source of regulation is within the person but is not integrated with the self. It is thus perceived as nonchoiceful, although the pressure and coercion stem from within rather than from without. A child who cleans her room because she would feel guilty, anxious, or uncomfortable if it were not clean is regulating through introjection.

A greater degree of internalization is seen in *identified regulation*. Here the person has identified with or personally taken on the value of the behavior and sees it as important for his or her own goals. The person has a sense of importance regarding the behavior and engages in it choicefully and without a sense of internal conflict. An example would be a child who cleans her room because she likes it clean so that she can find her things. Although cleaning her room is not fun or enjoyable, it serves her goals and is thus experienced as volitional.

Facilitating Internalization

The goals of parents are to help children move along the internalization continuum from external regulation, which requires prompts and pushes from parents, to self-regulation, in which the child willingly engages in the behavior because of his or her own goals. What brings about this movement? From a self-determination perspective, the movement toward self-regulation is an expression of individuals' innate tendencies to master their internal and external surroundings. Thus, the movement is intrinsically motivated. As such, it is based on an individual's inherent need for autonomy, competence, and relatedness. It then follows that internalization will be most likely when the environment satisfies these needs by supporting a child's autonomy rather than controlling the child's behavior. Controls may facilitate compliance but will undermine the active process of internalization, which must stem from the child. Internalization is something the child does and that comes from within. Control should thwart the internalization process.

However, although allowing children the freedom to pursue their interests without interference is paramount for intrinsic motivation, for internalization involvement and structure become even more key. Children will be most likely to internalize regulations when relatedness needs are met, meaning when they have a positive relationship with an involved, supportive parent. It is in this context that they are most likely to attend to and want to emulate the parent's behavior. Furthermore, when parents provide consistent structure—including guidelines, expectations, and rationales for their demands—children will have the information they need to internalize regulations. Without a clear rationale for performing a certain behavior children do not have the information to internalize. Behaviors must be meaningful to children, or they will not internalize their regulation. For example, rationales that do not make sense or that are above the child's ability to understand will not be internalized.

One example of such a rationale is going to bed on time. Parents often use the rationale that going to bed early is necessary because the child has something important to do in the morning. Parents can be highly autonomy supportive in providing this rationale, but if they analyze what it takes to understand this, they see that it may be beyond the comprehension of the young child. First, the child has to anticipate how he will feel tomorrow and link that to the activity he will pursue. Then he needs to connect something he is doing tonight with something that will happen tomorrow that is difficult itself to imagine. Although it is not harmful to provide this sensible, adult-oriented rationale, parents need to anticipate that this sort of reason may not be embraced by a 6- or 7-year-old. They may have to wait for internalization of this one.

"Because I said so" is also not a meaningful rationale, though we have all said it and it may let a child know that the parent means business. Further, it cannot be internalized by the child because it emphasizes parental control or power and thus is at odds with the child's need for autonomy.

Parenting and Internalization: Evidence Across Domains

What evidence is there that control undermines internalization? Research conducted across a variety of domains highlights the role of parental autonomy support in facilitating and parental control in undermining internalization.

SELF-REGULATION

Ryan and Connell (1989) developed a scale to assess children's levels of autonomy in their regulation of school behaviors. On this scale children report the reasons they engage in behaviors such as doing homework and classwork. *External* reasons include engaging in the behavior because of external contingencies or to avoid punishment (e.g., "I do my homework because I'll get in trouble if I don't"). *Introjected* reasons include behaving because the child would feel bad or unworthy if he or she did not (e.g., "I try to do well in school because I would feel bad about myself if I didn't"). *Identified* reasons include valuing learning and education (e.g., "I do my classwork because I want to understand the subject").

Before I describe how parental control is related to children's internalization for school behaviors, it is important that I make the point that the place at which students fall along this continuum has ramifications for behavior and adjustment in school. Children who do their schoolwork because they identify with the value of learning and education, for example, tend to cope more actively when they encounter difficulties in their work than do those who are less identified (Ryan & Connell, 1989). Children high in introjected regulation tend to report high levels of anxiety in school. These styles of regulation have consequences for children's behavior and adjustment.

Several studies have linked parental styles to children's self-regulation in a variety of domains. Grolnick and Ryan (1989) interviewed 114 mothers and fathers about how they motivate children for four behaviors, all extrinsically motivated: doing homework, going to bed on time, keeping their rooms clean, doing chores. They were asked a series of questions, such as:

"How do you motivate your child to _____?"

"What do you do when your child does a good job at _____?"

"What do you do when your child does a poor job at _____?"

"Do you have any rules or expectations about _____?"

On the basis of these interviews parents were rated according to how autonomy supportive versus controlling they were, how much consistent structure they provided, and how involved they were in their children's lives. These ratings were then related to a child's placement along the internalization continuum, indexed by the reasons provided for why they engaged in particular school behaviors. Results showed that parents who were rated as more autonomy supportive had children who reported more autonomous self-regulation in school than children of parents who were rated as more controlling. Furthermore, autonomy support was related to greater behavior regulation in school: Children of more autonomy supportive parents engaged in less disruptive behavior in the classroom and had better learning habits, such as study skills, than those of more controlling parents.

Another study, this time one that examined children's perceptions of their parents' autonomy support and involvement, showed that children who rated their parents as more autonomy supportive were more self-regulated in school; self-regulation, in turn, was associated with better school performance (Grolnick, Ryan, & Deci, 1991).

Deci et al. (1994) examined the effects of experimentally manipulated autonomy support and structure on internalization. The authors had college students engage in a relatively boring task: They had to press the space bar on a computer each time they saw a dot. Participants did this task in one of eight conditions, formed by the crossing of three facilitating conditions (i.e., the participants could have various combinations of 0, 1, 2, or 3 facilitating conditions). The first involved giving a meaningful rationale for the behavior: "The task is a concentration task used by air traffic controllers." The second was to provide an acknowledgment of the participants' feelings in finding the task boring. The third emphasized choice.

After doing the task under one of the eight conditions, participants were given a free-choice period in which they had the opportunity to do more of the task or to do other activities. Because the activity was boring, participants who chose to continue it would presumably be doing so because they had internalized the regulation of the activity. The students also reported on their feelings while doing this task. The results indicated that participants in conditions with more of the facilitating conditions spent more subsequent time on the activity than those with fewer of the conditions. This study demonstrates that providing a meaningful rationale, taking the participants' perspectives by validating their feelings about the task, and minimizing controls—in other words, autonomy support—facilitated internalization (Deci et al., 1994).

It is interesting that some of the participants in the less supportive conditions spent some free-choice time on the task (Deci et al., 1994). To see whether participants' experience in doing so differed from those in the more supportive conditions, Deci et al. (1994) correlated the amount of time spent in free choice and feelings of enjoyment, interest, and importance. For participants in the supportive conditions there was a positive correlation between time spent on the activity and reported interest, enjoyment, and feelings of freedom. For those in the nonsupportive conditions there was a negative correlation. Thus, in the nonsupportive conditions individuals who engaged in the activity did so for reasons other than wanting to. They presumably performed the behavior because they thought they should rather than because they thought it was important or worthwhile.

Deci et al.'s (1994) results suggest that if individuals do internalize regulations in less-than-optimal conditions, that internalization will likely take the form of introjection, replete with internal conflict and negative affect, rather than identification. Participants in the autonomy supportive conditions were more likely to have internalized the regulation more fully and thus engaged in it because of its perceived importance or interest. Bringing this back to parenting, the results also suggest that parents can promote partial internalization—for example, introjection—of regulations using somewhat controlling techniques. However, as we saw earlier, the guilt and other negative affects associated with introjected regulation make it a less adaptive way to regulate behavior.

A final line of research in our laboratory relevant to self-regulation has examined the regulation of emotion. The development of the ability to autonomously initiate and modulate emotion—for example, to calm down when you are upset, and initiate positive affect—is one of the hallmarks of toddlerhood. To examine the question of whether more controlling behavior on the part of parents would undermine the development of children's abilities to autonomously use strategies to calm themselves versus relying on caretakers, Grolnick, Bridges, and Connell (1996) identified strategies that toddlers use to regulate distress during a delay situation in which they had to wait to get an attractive toy. In one situation the mother was relatively passive, and in the other she was told that she could interact with the child in any way she liked. We were interested in the strategies mothers used to help their children wait and in how these strategies related to the children's abilities to modulate distress when they were on their own. Mothers used strategies such as actively engaging the child in an alternate activity and redirecting the child's attention by doing such things as giving the child an idea that might help him or her wait. Some mothers also physically comforted their children. Grolnick et al. (1996) also identified the initiator of the activity, whether it was mother or child. The results showed that, controlling for the level of distress in children, mothers who were actively engaged with the child, beyond the point at which the child was no longer distressed, were more distressed when they then had to regulate themselves. Mothers who sat back and allowed the child to initiate strategies while still being responsive had children who were less distressed when they were on their own. Thus, mothers who took responsibility for regulating the child's distress had children who were less able to regulate themselves. These children presumably had not internalized self-regulatory strategies. They were continuing to rely on their caretaker for assistance.

COMPLIANCE—NOW AND LATER

As I said earlier, getting children to change their behavior to conform immediately in one's presence—in other words, to comply—is not a difficult job. Building the kind of internal processes that lead children to follow rules and use good judgment in the absence of salient constraints is more challenging. There is evidence that more controlling techniques undermine children's compliance when adults are not present.

Hoffman (1960) showed that the more mothers used unqualified power assertion with children, the more those children became resistant to attempts by teachers and other children to influence them. Power assertion appears to result in children who do not bring their self-control into new settings. They also reject socialization attempts.

Lytton (1980) demonstrated a similar effect with young children. The focus of his study was on child outcomes of internalization and compliance, which were based on parents' ratings of whether they had to remind the child to obey and whether the child exhibited self-restraint. Using observations of mother–child interactions, Lytton showed that mothers who were more controlling and scolded their children frequently had children with poorer internalization scores than children of mothers who scolded less and who helped their children do things independently.

Kochanska and her colleagues (e.g., Kochanska, 1995; Kochanska & Aksan, 1995), in searching for the origins of conscience in children, reasoned that rather than seeing compliance and internalization as separate and distinct, one could find the origins of internalization in early compliance—but not just any compliance. Kochanska (1995) differentiated between two types: situational and committed. Children were rated high in *situational compliance* when they were cooperative but required the mother's sustained or repeated controls to maintain cooperation or when they seemed on the verge of noncompliance. By contrast, in *committed compliance* the child appears to endorse or embrace the parent's agenda as his or her own. The child cooperates without parental intervention or even repeats the rule or guideline. For example, in a mother–child task in which children were prohibited from playing with a set of toys, situationally compliant children hovered around the toys and had to be repeatedly told not to touch them. Children rated as committed did not have to be reminded, even saying things like "We can't touch these."

Kochanska and her colleagues (e.g., Kochanska, Aksan, & Koenig, 1995; Kochanska, 1997) have found links between these different forms of compliance shown early on and later internalization. Kochanska, Aksan, and Koenig (1995) found that children high in committed compliance at age 2 years were less likely to "cheat" in the absence of adult surveillance at age 4. In other words, committed compliance may be a precursor to internalization. What is interesting here is the kind of parenting that facilitates committed compliance. Kochanska and Aksan (1995) showed that committed compliance was more likely when parent–child relationships were characterized by high mutual positive affect. A positive relationship between parent and child characterized by mutual respect and positive feelings goes a long way in facilitating children's desire to please the parent and follow directions. Furthermore, mothers who used more gentle rather than power-assertive discipline had children with higher committed compliance. In another study, Kochanska (1997) identified parents and children who appeared to have a "mutual positive orientation." In dyads with this orientation the parent and child were most responsive to each other, and they engaged in mutual positive affect. They were also highly cooperative with each other. Furthermore, in such dyads mothers tended not to use either physical or verbal power assertion, and parents were high in perspective taking. Both of these characteristics—low use of control and high perspective taking— are characteristic of autonomy supportive parenting. A mutual positive orientation was associated with higher levels of internalization, as assessed by observing the children when they received prohibitions from their mothers in the laboratory. Kochanska (1997) also saw this in the children's reluctance to violate rules and by mothers reporting that their children were more internalized— in other words, more likely to follow rules without reminders—at home.

Attribution theory has spawned much of the research on compliance in the absence of surveillance. The attributional framework assumes that individuals are meaning makers and search for causes for their behavior. These causes, then, have implications for guiding future behavior. When searching for causes, people focus both on external causes, such as rewards or strong constraints, that can justify engaging in a particular behavior, and internal causes, such as one's personality or values. When there is strong external justification for a person's behavior the person will discount internal factors in favor of the external: "I didn't cheat because the penalty was so high." On the contrary, when the external justification is small, a person will attribute the cause to him- or herself: "I didn't cheat; I must be an honest person." When the dispositional attribution is made, the person will be more likely to behave in accord with it the next time.

Applying this reasoning to the issue of internalization, Lepper (1983) described the *minimal-sufficiency principle*, according to which the internalization of a regulation is most likely when the social control surrounding the behavior is just sufficient to elicit the behavior but is minimally coercive so that the child cannot attribute his or her compliance to external constraints. If parents wish a child to behave according to rules or regulations in the absence of adult surveillance, they should apply just enough pressure to get the child to engage in that new behavior yet not so much that the pressure rather than the rule is salient. In short, apply enough pressure to be sure the child will comply, but not so much that the child attributes that compliance to pressure.

In a number of studies testing these ideas Lepper (1983) compared the effects of weak and stronger sanctions on children's deviation in the absence of adult supervision. In his classic "forbidden toy" laboratory studies (e.g., Lepper, 1973), children received either mild or severe threats about the consequences of playing with a forbidden toy. Those who received the mild threat were most likely to devalue the toys in a subsequent session. Most important, those children were most likely to resist temptation in an entirely new situation 2 weeks later. Lepper concluded that compliance in the presence of strong constraints undermines internalization while compliance in the presence of weak constraints facilitates internalization.

In an interesting variant of this paradigm, Lepper and Gilovich (1982) tested strategies that they believed would facilitate children's compliance with an initial request and with a similar request made 2 weeks later. In one situation they used a fantasy transformation strategy, in which children were told to imagine another context and meaning for the situation (e.g., pretend you are a robot picking up moon rocks). In another condition, children created goals for themselves (e.g., see how fast you can pick up the blocks). Children in the fantasy condition and those in the goal condition were more likely to comply with a request to pick up tennis balls 2 weeks later than those in the no-fantasy and no-goal conditions. Lepper and Gilovich suggested that the effects of the two strategy conditions are due to the fact that, relative to the no-strategy conditions, the children were focused more on the activity and less on the external constraint. Later, the children attribute their participation in the activity more to themselves than to adult coercion and thus subsequently behaved in a more compliant manner.

Consistent with this work, Grusec and Redler (1980) suggested that parents who want their children to comply in their absence induce the children to make purposeful attribution errors by attributing the compliance to the children and not to the inducements. For example, a parent might say "You did that because you're a helpful person" when the child does the dishes, even though in reality the parent did apply some subtle persuasion. In the future the child presumably will be more likely to do the dishes without reminding.

In many ways the work stemming from an attributional framework is consistent with that derived from self-determination theory. Both stress that internalization will be forestalled by strong external controls. Both recommend minimizing control to maximize internalization. However, the mechanisms behind internalization in the two theories are quite different and lead to different conclusions about the effectiveness of various parenting strategies. First, if the attributional theory is correct, then children go through a fairly sophisticated process of inferring the causality of their behavior in the process of internalizing regulations. For the mechanism to work, children need to search for the causes of their behavior, identify environmental and internal causes, and use the principle of discounting internal causes if the external ones are strong. If this is the case, parental controls should only undermine internalization in children sophisticated enough to use these processes. Several investigators have shown that children do not use the discounting principle until about 8 years of age (e.g., Karniol & Ross, 1976; Smith, 1975). Thus, parental control should not undermine internalization for the first 6–7 years of life. It is only later that parents have to worry about the use of controls.

The self-determination approach is a more experiential theory in contrast to attribution theory, which is more strictly cognitive. From a self-determination framework, external controls, such as rewards, threats, and other pressures, lead people directly to feeling coerced, that their behavior is initiated from without. No inferential process is needed. Individuals do not need to look back on their behavior to determine its cause; rather, they perceive its cause from their own inner experience. Research suggests that children do not have to have sophisticated cognitive processes to be undermined by control and, in fact, Grolnick et al. (1984) found that the undermining effects of control are apparent as early as 1 year of age. If this is so, then the roots of individual differences in internalization may be seen early. This is consistent with Kochanska's work, reviewed earlier.

Second, attribution theory does not distinguish between different types of internalization. The dependent variable in many studies is whether children deviate in the absence of adult surveillance; in other words, the dependent variable is compliance. Yet children comply for many reasons and as the result of different attributions. One child may refrain from touching a forbidden object in a strained way, struggling with internal conflict, feeling tempted and yet suppressing those feelings, whereas another child may do so smoothly and comfortably. Children may attribute their behavior to guilt avoidance as well as to dispositions or values, all of which are internal factors. Attributions that are internally controlling or pressuring would feel controlled rather than autonomous.

Finally, attributional approaches speak of avoiding strong controls but are less explicit about what the replacement would be. As we discussed, from a self-determination viewpoint subtle or covert controls can sometimes be just as pressuring as stronger controls. Misleading children with subtle manipulation may be perceived as controlling. I suggest that external control should be replaced not with covert control but with autonomy support. Providing rationales and clear consequences for behavior in the context of choice, acknowledgment of feelings, and minimization of pressure should facilitate the active process of internalization.

This view is consistent with recent arguments made by Baumrind (1996) that internalization will be facilitated with active parenting techniques rather than a nonconfrontational, passive approach by parents. In her view, both permissive parents who accept all impulses and thus avoid confrontation, and authoritarian parents who suppress dissent, shield children from having to interact with others when it comes to unwelcome demands. Children need the opportunity to negotiate, make choices, and be given the opportunity to suffer the consequences of their choices. In autonomy supportive, structured homes parents do not hide their agendas but put them on the table and open themselves up to discussion and negotiation around those agendas.

MORAL AND PROSOCIAL DEVELOPMENT

The study of morality in children looks at the development of standards of conduct considered ethical within a culture. It includes areas such as judging right from wrong, inhibiting behaviors that harm others, and displaying behaviors that are sensitive to others' needs.

Children's moral and prosocial development have been conceptualized as issues of internalization. Children presumably move along a developmental continuum ranging from more heteronomous to more autonomous morality. Kohlberg's (1976) scheme suggests that children move in a stagelike manner from control of conduct being external to more internal. At Level 1, the child is controlled by avoiding external punishment or the provision of a reward. At Level 2, the child is concerned with conforming to expectations of others and maintaining the social order. At this point, control comes from within, but it is more duty based than value based. At Level 3, conduct is controlled through internal principles. Standards have been internalized such that they are experienced as one's own, and the emphasis is more on what is right than on what looks good.

Eisenberg (1986) similarly described a continuum of prosocial behaviors, that is, those that benefit or sustain others. In her conceptualization the young child is hedonistic. In the child's prosocial acts he or she is focused on external pressures, on the avoidance of punishment and the attainment of rewards or preservation of his or her own interests. The elementary school child's reasoning reflects his or her concern for approval; he or she wants to be "good." Beginning in late elementary school, children begin to use reasoning based on abstract principles and concern for the welfare of others. Such concern represents more internalized reasoning.

Although both Kohlberg's (1976) and Eisenberg's (1986) theories predict that children will move further toward autonomous morality as they develop, there are also strong individual differences in where children are at any age. Is there evidence that children's moral development is enhanced by autonomy supportive rather than controlling parenting? In a series of studies conducted in the early 1970s, Hoffman (e.g., 1970) showed that power assertive parenting was associated with low moral development. In particular, a moral orientation based on fear of external detection and punishment was associated with parenting characterized by high physical force, material deprivation, or the threat of these. Higher moral development was associated with techniques that point out the consequences of the child's behavior for others, either di-rectly—for example, "If you keep pushing him, he'll fall down and cry"—or in-directly—for example, "Don't yell at him. He was only trying to help." Hoffman described these techniques as *inductions*. Inductions are explanations or reasons parents use that appeal to the child's concern for others. Hoffman posited that other-oriented induction is especially important for moral development. From a self-determination viewpoint, induction gives children information they need to internalize moral codes. Forceful styles, on the other hand, keep moral orien-tation tied to these threats and prevent internalization.

Sally Powers (1982; Powers, Hauser, Schwartz, Noam, & Jacobson, 1983) ex-amined parents' behavior during family discussions of moral dilemmas. Her findings showed, in contrast to what one might intuitively predict, that it was not how cognitively stimulating the parents' discussions were that predicted high levels of moral development in children but rather how supportive versus interfering the parents were during these discussions. Parents who were more supportive and who were less likely to interfere in their children's communica-tions had children who were more advanced in their moral reasoning.

Walker and Taylor (1991), responding to earlier arguments that peers rather than parents are responsible for children's moral development, suggested that the way parents discuss moral issues with their children determines how the chil-dren's moral reasoning progressed. Coming from a cognitive–developmental per-spective, they suggested that discussion could induce cognitive conflict, or disequilibrium, that children would then reflect on, resolve, and use to come to their own opinions. But what kind of discussion? Would that make a difference?

Two studies focused on this issue. Walker and Taylor (1991) looked at chil-dren's moral reasoning level and then conducted a follow-up study 2 years later. They also had parents and children interact in a discussion of a moral dilemma and assessed their interaction styles. The discussion style that resulted in the greatest increases in moral reasoning over the 2-year time span was the one in which parents elicited the child's opinion, asked clarifying questions, and checked the child's understanding. That style is consistent with an autonomy supportive stance in which the parent attempts to take the child's perspective and support his or her initiations. In contrast, a style that directly challenges and criticizes the child and one in which the parent provides his or her opinions—described as resembling lecturing—were associated with lesser increases in moral reasoning over the 2 years. Conceptually, these styles are controlling.

CONCLUSIONS

The evidence suggests that, across a variety of children's ages and in a multitude of domains, when parents use techniques that exert pressure, that take responsibility for children's behavior, and that manipulate compliance, they undermine their own goals. Children are less likely to take responsibility for their own behavior and are less likely to take on the parents' values. Perhaps it makes sense for parents to use more power assertive techniques in situations that do not have ramifications beyond the immediate time. They can save the autonomy supportive techniques for long-term goals.

It is interesting that parents intuitively believe that pressure will be more useful in isolated situations. When Kuczynski (1984) led mothers to believe that children's immediate compliance was important, mothers used simple power assertive techniques, such as orders or threats. However, mothers who were led to believe that compliance that would persist in their absence was key were more likely to rely on reasoning, positive character attributions, and conversation during the compliance task. Similarly, mothers of 4- to 8-year–olds reported that they used more power assertion in situations in which immediate control was important—for example, when the child was arguing with his or her peers or was ignoring a call to dinner. These mothers reported using more reasoning and explanations in situations that had long-term implications for their children and for which internal control would be important, such as stealing from the mother's purse or teasing an elderly man.

The problem here, of course, is the fine line between incidents that have long-term implications and those that do not. Screaming at your child for not coming down to dinner may seem like an isolated situation, but it is easily generalized as "things Mother asks me to do." The need to stop fights between siblings obviously requires immediate strategies, because children can get hurt, yet this is also a situation in which children can learn about dealing with others' feelings and being patient and sharing. These traits are obviously fundamentally moral and attitudinal.

As I argued early on, the climate of the family, whether characterized by respect for the child's autonomy or focused on obedience, can determine whether the same techniques will be effective. In the context of controlling parenting, the explanations parents provide may not be heard or may be perceived as lectures rather than rationales. For these reasons, an autonomy supportive approach, characterized by mutual respect, rules, and regulations, conveyed with choice and the minimization of pressure, is most likely to facilitate a child's overall adjustment and well-being.

⚜6⚜

Control in Context

A number of years ago, I was describing at my research group meeting some of my ideas about controlling parenting. Out of the corner of my eye I saw a befuddled look on one of my students' faces. When I asked Juliet what was confusing, she explained that her parents, who grew up in China, did many of the things that would seem to be considered controlling. For example, she was not allowed to go to sleepovers even though all the girls in her class were going. "You don't sleep at somebody else's house," she was told the first time she asked. She never asked again. When the family moved to Massachusetts, Juliet wanted to buy clothes like the other girls. Her parents said no. "I looked different from everybody," she said. "The interesting thing, though, is that I never questioned my parents' actions. I knew they loved me. I knew that the family came first. I would never have thought of their actions as infringing on my autonomy."

Thus far I have argued that controlling techniques and styles detract from children's motivation to pursue activities they love. Furthermore, in controlling environments children are less likely to move toward greater self-regulation for schoolwork, chores, and other activities that do not interest them spontaneously. My basic assumption has been that human beings have innate needs for autonomy. They need to experience themselves as initiators, or agents in their lives. They also have innate needs for competence and relatedness. Conditions that facilitate the fulfillment of those needs increase motivation and adjustment. Controlling parental environments thwart a child's innate needs for autonomy, thereby sapping the child's motivation and agency. Because the work my research group conducts is based on a theory involving human needs, we presume that it will hold for all children and parents. It should also hold across cultural groups, family types, and age ranges. This component of the theory is rather strong. Readers might ask whether there is evidence that this is, indeed, true. Can researchers provide evidence that parental control is detrimental to all children? Or is it possible that the effects of control differ for various cultural or ethnic groups or for families in different circumstances?

The view that autonomy supportive rather than controlling parenting is "effective" is certainly at odds with the current zeitgeist of cultural relativity, which claims that there is no such thing as universally "good" parenting but rather that good parenting depends on the culture. A culturally relative position suggests that groups have different values and that it is impossible to tell what is going to be effective in families without knowing the specific values of a culture. In addressing this position, a first question pertains to whether the same types of parenting—for example, autonomy supportive or authoritative—have the same effects in different cultural groups. A second related issue with which researchers have grappled is whether the dimension itself—say, that of autonomy support—is the same in different cultural contexts. For example, those who are products of culture in the 50 states can typically understand and respond to questions about whether or not they value obedience in children. They can easily express their attitudes toward their roles as the ultimate authorities. Most parents in the United States have opinions regarding whether they believe children should obey parents without question or whether children should be encouraged to express their feelings and points of view. However, some theorists challenge the idea that the American notion of obedience translates into the same concept in Asian cultures (Chao, 1994). In other words, when parents from Asian cultures use the term *obedience* or endorse questionnaire items on the value of obedience, they may mean something different than when U.S. parents do the same. The idea of the cultural equivalence of concepts is crucial if one is to ask whether the same parenting practices are effective across cultures.

In an attempt to address these issues I first discuss research that has asked whether findings on the effects of parental control hold across different cultural groups. Then, taking into account these findings, I explore the possibility that our concepts and measures may have different meaning in different groups. Finally, I ask whether the meanings parents in various cultures attribute to parenting dimensions may explain disparate findings on the effects of parenting across these varied groups.

DOES CONTROL HAVE DETRIMENTAL EFFECTS ACROSS CULTURAL GROUPS?

To date, few studies have examined the effects of the same parenting practices across different cultural groups. One of the difficulties in asking questions about the consistency of findings across different groups is that studies addressing such questions have to be extremely large, which means they must include hundreds, perhaps thousands, of children. This number is necessary to ensure that each group has an adequate sample size. Two studies that included large samples of children have addressed questions of cross-group consistency.

Before I review these studies it is important to acknowledge that when researchers divide families into groups the resulting groups are far from perfectly formed. At times, families are categorized by race, at other times by country of origin or language. Thus the delineations along which families are divided can differ between studies or even within the same study. Furthermore, within many of the categories there is great diversity. For example, within a Latino-American group one may find families who are Puerto Rican, Dominican, and Mexican. In an Asian group one may find individuals of Chinese, Japanese, Korean, Filipino, or Southeast Asian descent. Each of these groups may have different cultural practices. However, even noting these imperfect categorizations, researchers are beginning to address important questions about parenting across groups.

The first study was conducted by Dornbusch et al. (1987). They surveyed 7,836 adolescents enrolled in six high schools in California. Students were divided into four groups on the basis of their reported ethnic background: Asian, African American, Hispanic, White.

Dornbusch et al.'s (1987) survey assessed three parenting style indexes that roughly conformed to Baumrind's (1967) three styles of parenting. The authoritarian scale measured the extent to which parents present themselves as ultimate authorities and discourage give and take; for example, parents tell the youth not to argue with adults because parents are correct and should not be questioned. In our conceptualization, these parents would be controlling. The authoritative index stresses open communication and the valuing of children's ideas and output. For example, parents may emphasize that everyone should help with decisions in the family or admit that sometimes the child knows more than the parents do. Again, within our framework, this type of parenting would be autonomy supportive. The permissive scale denotes a hands-off approach on the part of parents; for example, parents don't care if children get good or bad grades, or there are no rules concerning television watching. Within our conceptualization, this means that parents lack structure, although no information on control versus autonomy support is contained in the scale.

Two questions can be asked regarding these data. First, are there differences among groups in children's reporting of their parents' adherence to the various approaches? Second, are the approaches related to children's outcomes—say, school achievement—in the same way across different groups? These are two different questions which, as we will see later, are not necessarily connected.

With regard to the first question, there were group differences in children's reporting of parental styles in Dornbusch et al.'s (1987) study. In particular, Asian, African American, and Hispanic families were higher on the authoritarian index than were White families. Families of Asian, Hispanic, and African American adolescents were lower on the authoritative index than were White families. For permissiveness, compared to Whites, African Americans were lower, Hispanics were higher, and Asians were slightly higher. Thus, there is some evidence that different cultural groups endorse different parenting styles.

The second question asks about relations between the three indexes of parenting and children's grades. Across ethnic groups, authoritarian and permissive styles were associated with lower grades, and an authoritative style was associated with higher grades. However, there were some differences in the strength of the correlations. For Asians, the correlation between grades and authoritative parenting was small, although the negative relation between authoritarian parenting and grades was more robust. In general, in Dornbusch et al.'s large-scale study authoritative parenting was associated with positive outcomes, and authoritarian and permissive styles were associated with negative outcomes, although there were some differences in the strength of these relations. I return to these findings, particularly for the Asian families, later.

A second study, conducted by Lamborn, Dornbusch, and Steinberg (1996), examined an issue related to parenting style: the frequency of different types of decision making in the home. The authors surveyed 3,597 students, dividing them into four groups: African American, Asian American, Hispanic American, and European American. Students reported on how frequently decisions in the home tended to be (a) joint between parents and adolescent; (b) unilateral parent, in that parents decide without adolescent input; or (c) unilateral adolescent, where the adolescent decides without parental input. Although joint decision making would be most consistent with an autonomy supportive style, unilateral parent with a controlling style, and unilateral adolescent with a lack of structure, decision making is only one aspect of parenting and thus Lamborn et al. (1996) focused on a narrower dimension than parental style.

The results of Lamborn et al.'s (1996) study are fairly consistent with those of Dornbusch et al. (1987), with some exceptions. Across groups, unilateral adolescent decision making consistently predicted negative outcomes, including lower academic competence, and more involvement in deviant activities. Thus, adolescents whose parents had a hands-off, uninvolved approach in which they chose their own friends, classes, and curfews, had more trouble than other children. These results echo earlier findings that highlight the need for parents to be "in control" and involved in their children's lives. By contrast, joint decision making was associated with higher academic competence and more positive psychosocial development among African American, Hispanic American, and European American youth. Unilateral parental decision making was associated with negative characteristics for European American youth. This style had no relation to outcomes for Asian American and Hispanic American youth, and it had a somewhat positive impact on African American youth.

Thus, although there was general consistency in findings across groups in the Lamborn et al. (1996) study, there also were anomalies, such as the evidence that unilateral parental decisions did not have an impact, or even showed a positive result, for some groups. A possible explanation is that the meaning of decision-making practices may be different for some groups than for others. One hypothesis is that families of ethnic minorities live in poorer and more dangerous neighborhoods, and as a result, these parents need to be more controlling than parents in middle-class neighborhoods. Let's look at that theory.

COMMUNITY CONTEXT: THE "DANGEROUS-NEIGHBORHOOD" HYPOTHESIS

The dangerous-neighborhood hypothesis suggests that an autonomy supportive approach may not be the best in an environment that is dangerous. Instead, a more controlling, authoritarian approach is more effective. The reasoning is thus: Children who live in poorer and more dangerous communities with higher crime rates and higher rates of drug and gang involvement (Duncan, 1991) are at risk for engaging in risky behaviors or being the victims of such behaviors. In such contexts authoritarian parenting serves a protective function. Using this reasoning, parents should restrict children more to assure the children's safety and well-being. A controlling stance would be less detrimental in this context than it would be in other situations. What is the evidence for the dangerous-neighborhood hypothesis? If this hypothesis were supported by data, this would suggest that control would be more positive for some groups of ethnic minorities living in poorer and more dangerous neighborhoods than for majority families.

One of the studies frequently cited to support the dangerous-neighborhood hypothesis is that conducted by Baldwin, Baldwin, and Cole (1990). These authors followed a group of children from before they were born—during their mothers' pregnancies—through the children's early adolescence. When the children were between ages 12 and 14 years, the researchers conducted interviews with them and their families. The families were divided into high- and low-risk groups on the basis of their socioeconomic circumstances, level of parental education, minority status, and absence of the father. The groupings were then divided on the basis of the child's competence, as measured by IQ and school achievement, into successful and unsuccessful groups. Mothers and fathers were interviewed extensively about their parenting, and particularly about the rules and regulations in the home and their values for their children. On the basis of the interviews, parents were rated on several dimensions. One was how restrictive the parents were. For example, parents who required their child to be home after school would be rated as more restrictive than parents whose child just had to let them know where he or she was. A second rated dimension was clarity of rules. How well did the child know what the rules were? A third issue was democracy of policy. Was the child consulted when parents established these policies? Finally, parents were evaluated regarding whether they provided justification for their policies. Did parents explain to their children why the rules were important?

There were some differences between the high- and low-risk groups in their parenting. Families from the high-risk group were more restrictive and less democratic than those in the low-risk group. Most interesting, however, is whether and how these characteristics correlated with competence in children in the high- and low-risk groups. Baldwin et al. (1990) found that restrictiveness was associated with positive outcomes for children in the high-risk group but negatively associated with outcomes for those children at low risk. Among the high-risk group, parents who were more restrictive had children who were doing *better* in school and who had higher IQs. Conversely, in the low-risk group, the more restrictive the parent, the less competent the child. Does this mean that control is good in risky environments?

Not really. The other characteristics of parenting that Baldwin et al. (1990) examined complete the story. Although restrictiveness was "good" in the high-risk group and "bad" in the low-risk group, parents of cognitively competent children in *both* groups were more democratic in the way they developed their rules, and they provided more justification for their rules, than parents of less competent children. Furthermore, both high- and low-risk families that were successful endorsed a low value of obedience and a high value of responsibility in their children. Restrictiveness, defined as how numerous and how circumscribed the rules were, does seem to have different consequences for children in risky and nonrisky environments. However, when rules are conveyed in a controlling manner, with little room for child input or problem solving, this same quality of restrictiveness appeared to have negative consequences for children in risky and nonrisky situations. The dangerous-neighborhood hypothesis obviously did not hold for controlling parents in this study.

Successful high-risk families in Baldwin et al.'s (1990) study had clear and strong rules but were democratic in their administration of these rules. In our conceptualization, successful families would be labeled high in structure and high in autonomy supportiveness and, by contrast, low in controlling behavior. Rather than being at odds with our general thesis, Baldwin et al.'s results are quite consistent. Instead of showing that controlling behavior is sometimes good, this outcome makes the important point that the optimal level of structure—in other words, being "in control"—may be a function of the family's circumstances. In dangerous contexts, the need for rules and guidelines that are clear and strictly enforced is certainly even higher than it is in more privileged neighborhoods. Although middle-class families may be able to get away with lax rules and less-than-comprehensive monitoring, the stakes in dangerous areas are too high. The children are too vulnerable. Structure is clearly crucial in high-risk circumstances. For example, one mother from the successful high-risk group walked her child to school each day and met the child after school each afternoon. When the child complained that the mother did not trust her, the mother said that it was not the child but the "weirdos" in the neighborhood whom she mistrusted. Baldwin et al.'s study also supports the idea that even in high-risk neighborhoods there are benefits to open communication, joint problem solving, and valuation of a child's individuality as well as his or her input. For children who are faced with difficult environments and who must negotiate peer pressure and the sometimes-coercive opportunities for engaging in deviant activities, the development of self-regulation and responsibility—both outcomes of autonomy supportive parenting—are just as necessary, if not more so, than they are for children of advantage.

Incidentally, Lamborn et al. (1996), who grouped children by ethnicity, also divided them according to whether they lived in more and less advantaged neighborhoods. Unilateral parental decision making did not have more favorable effects in less advantaged circumstances—a fact that also refutes the dangerous-neighborhood hypothesis.

Although there is little evidence that a parent's controllingness is beneficial in dangerous contexts, there is no doubt that the circumstances within which parents function lead them to provide more or less control. For example, parents from more disadvantaged circumstances tend to use more controlling techniques (Kelley, Sanchez-Hucles, & Walker, 1993), and these findings cross racial barriers (Hess & Shipman, 1965). As I discuss at length in the next chapter, the effects of financial stress, unemployment, and scarce resources can certainly undermine parents' capacities to provide autonomy supportive parenting. Furthermore, parents' fears for their children also may play a role in their levels of control. For example, Kelley (1988) found that mothers who were worried about child victimization stressed obedience more than those who were less worried. In our own work, which I discuss later, parents who perceived a more threatening world for their children were found to use more controlling childrearing strategies than those who perceived the world to be less threatening. However, saying that the environment in which families live and their perceptions of it can affect their controllingness is quite different from saying that controlling techniques are preferable. Furthermore, such blanket statements about groups such as Latinos or disadvantaged families ignore the fact that within any population there is wide variation in the techniques that are used and in people's attitudes toward child obedience. Kelley, Power, and Wimbush (1992) found a wide range of disciplinary practices among low-income African American mothers. Although we claim that autonomy support is preferable to control, that very same control is an understandable response to difficult circumstances. Furthermore, even though researchers have identified differences between groups of parents, all parents within those groups obviously are not alike. There are clearly individual differences within every group, with parents displaying a full range of styles.

We are left, however, with some unexplained findings. Why in Dornbusch et al.'s (1987) study was there no effect of authoritarian parenting for Asian families? This quandary brings us to the second question posed at the beginning of this chapter: Can it be that some of the concepts are not equivalent in different cultures?

ETHNICITY: CULTURAL VARIATION WITHIN AND ACROSS GROUPS

There has been a great focus on school achievement in Asian cultures as Asian American students in the United States have outperformed their White, African American, and Hispanic American counterparts in school (Steinberg, 1996; Sue & Okazaki, 1990). They are also more engaged in school, as evidenced by the fact that they spend more time on homework. They also report that they work at higher levels of attention and concentration in class (Steinberg, 1996) than do European American, Hispanic American, or African American children. How does this student profile fit with the concept of the authoritarian parent that was seen in some of the studies reviewed thus far and that is a stereotype in the literature?

In fact, several studies have found that Chinese parents are more controlling (Chiu, 1987; Lin & Fu, 1990), or authoritarian with their children and that they value obedience more highly than do other groups (Dornbusch et al., 1987). Chao (1994) questioned, however, whether these parenting concepts such as authoritarianism, mean the same thing to Asians as they do to European Americans and whether there are completely different dimensions that are relevant to Asian families. A closer look at the doctrines that Asian families may follow illustrates this point.

Chao (1994) pointed out that many of the descriptions of Asian family practices rely on the doctrine of Confucianism. The Confucian tradition stresses roles that are structured and hierarchical, emphasizing that each party must honor the requirements and responsibilities of his or her role. The parental job, hierarchically at the top of the family's structure, is to provide training to the children in appropriate or expected behaviors—such as performing well in school. However, although the concept of training may evoke notions of controlling behaviors in Western culture, the concept of training, or *Chiao sun*, in China includes an extremely nurturing environment. Under this doctrine, when the child is very young the parent attends to the child's every need. As the child ages, the parent provides high levels of support and encouragement to achieve. Thus, the environment is highly involved and extremely supportive. High standards are maintained. Furthermore, Chao explained, the standards are intended not to dominate but to protect a vulnerable and innocent child and to assure family harmony. Another standard, *guan*, literally means "to govern." However, in China this has a positive connotation. It can mean "to care for" or even "to love," as well as "to govern." Thus, parents high in *guan* may be experienced by Chinese children as loving and caring first and foremost.

The different interpretation of parental practices is illustrated by the example of my student, Juliet, at the beginning of the chapter. Whereas a child of American parents may have experienced the strict, unexplained practices as controlling, Juliet did not. The practices were embedded in a context in which their meaning was different and did not convey pressure. I spoke to Juliet recently. She is now married to a man of Western descent and is the mother of two young girls. In looking back on her childhood through a new lens, she does see herself as having missed out on important experiences of childhood because of her parents' control. She plans to do things quite differently with her own children.

Different interpretations by children of the same parenting practices also are illustrated in a study of Korean youth conducted by Rohner and Pettengill (1985), who focused on children's differing perceptions of parenting practices. Other studies conducted in European American cultures have typically found negative correlations between measures of parental warmth and controllingness. In other words, among European American children, the more controlling they rate their parents, the less warm they perceive them to be. By contrast in Rohner and Pettengill's sample of 125 Korean adolescents the results were reversed. The more controlling that children rated their parents, the warmer they rated them. Thus, some of the same behaviors engaged in by European mothers would be perceived by Korean children as acts of love and caring rather than as efforts to dominate and control. Furthermore, there is evidence that Asian and Latin American children themselves value their duty to assist, respect, and support their families more than do their peers from European backgrounds (Fuligni, Tseng, & Lam, 1999). In other words, they perceive the hierarchical system not as one that by nature is controlling but rather as a system that has meaning for connecting the family. It is one that they themselves value. The system itself may not be inherently controlling either to children or adolescents.

Chao's (1994) arguments and Rohner and Pettengill's (1985) findings make the important point that different cultures may have varying concepts and dimensions of parenting. It becomes extremely important for researchers to be sure that there is equivalence in their constructs if they are to make statements about parenting that cross groups. It is not enough to translate measures into different languages—if that were possible. If the meaning of the practice itself is different, then the results of the group comparison will be unintelligible.

Putting cultural meanings of our concepts of control aside for the moment, we can ask a question. Is there evidence—gathered with researchers' perhaps-imperfect measures—that authoritarianism per se is *positive* in Asian cultures? Chen, Dong, and Zhou (1997) studied 304 second-grade children in Beijing, China. Parents filled out a Chinese version of Block's (1981) Child Rearing Practices Report, which provides indexes of authoritarian and authoritative styles. Authoritative parenting consists of rational guidance, reasoning, encouragement of autonomy, and parent–child communication. The authoritarian items assess the use of physical punishment, verbal reprimands, power assertive strategies, and discouragement of a child's emotional expression and opinions.

Chen et al. (1997) related parenting on these dimensions to a number of child outcomes, including peer relations, behavior in the classroom, academic achievement, and leadership. In this sample of Chinese families, the more authoritarian the parenting styles, the more aggression–disruption the children displayed in the classroom, and the less the children were preferred by their peers. Their school achievement was lower as well. On the other hand, the more authoritative the style of parents, the more well-liked the children were by peers, and the higher their school achievement was. These children were less disruptive in the classroom. In short, using the parenting characteristics derived from the U.S. research, the results are highly consistent. The more controlling the parents, the lower the child's competence.

There is one interesting difference in Chen et al.'s (1997) study: For both mothers and fathers, the more authoritarian the parent, the less shy the child. More authoritative parenting resulted in higher levels of shyness. This result is the opposite of the finding in Western culture that authoritarian practices are positively associated with shy, restrained, and reticent behavior (e.g., Baumrind, 1967; Mills & Rubin, 1993). Chen et al. suggested that the different outcomes are the consequence of the different meaning of shy–inhibited behavior in the two cultures. Whereas shy–anxious behavior in Western culture is considered immature and a sign of social incompetence, in Chinese culture shyness is equated with high social competence. It is a desirable trait. It is important that one understands what is considered competent in a given culture. Although competence can indeed be culturally relative, the positive connections between autonomy supportive parenting and positive outcomes appears to hold across cultures.

Chirkov and Ryan (2001) conducted a study that focused on Russian families. Unlike Chen et al.'s (1997) study, in which there was no attempt to ascertain whether there was equivalence in the way Chinese and U.S. parents would interpret questionnaire items, Chirkov and Ryan made the equivalence of concepts of autonomy support and control an explicit focus. They asked high school students in Russia and the United States to complete questionnaires. The 120 Russian and 146 U.S. students were asked to evaluate their parents' and teachers' levels of autonomy support versus control during interactions. The Russian culture is an interesting one on which to focus, because it has long been viewed as authoritarian. According to Ispa (1995), the culture has traditionally fostered values consistent with its long history of totalitarianism, loyalty, obedience, group-mindedness, and conformity. Given this, Chirkov and Ryan expected that, overall, Russian adolescents would describe their teachers and parents as more controlling than would students from the United States. In addition, given the researchers' theoretical reliance on self-determination theory, they expected that more controlling styles in parents and teachers would be associated with negative outcomes for children. They also anticipated that children would not have as strong a feeling of well-being and that there would be more external regulation in both cultures.

Chirkov and Ryan (2001) translated measures of autonomy support versus control into Russian and administered the questionnaires to students in the city of Yarslovl. As a first step, they used sophisticated analytic techniques called *means and covariance structure analyses* (Little, 1997) to determine whether the measured constructs were comparable across the two cultures. They concluded that there were no significant differences in the constructs between the two groups. U.S. adolescents appeared to interpret the parenting items in ways similar to that of Russians. Next, Chirkov and Ryan related the parent and teacher constructs to teenagers' outcomes.

The results indicated that the more autonomy supportive adolescents perceived their parents to be, the greater their mental health (Chirkov & Ryan, 2001). The effects of autonomy support to control were virtually identical in the two groups. Furthermore, for both groups, students who perceived their parents as more autonomy supportive and less controlling were less likely to rely on external contingencies such as rewards or punishments for their school motivation. They were more likely to do their schoolwork because they valued learning. Students who saw their teachers as more autonomy supportive and less controlling showed more identified regulation and more intrinsic motivation. Although the Russian adolescents perceived their parents and teachers to be more controlling than did their U.S. counterparts, the effects of autonomy support versus control were quite similar. Chirkov and Ryan's (2001) study provides strong support for the notion that controlling parenting is associated with more negative outcomes for children across cultural context.

WHY ARE THERE STRONG FEELINGS ABOUT THE UNIVERSAL BENEFITS OF AUTONOMY SUPPORT?

There is a reluctance on the part of researchers and theorists to accept the overall positive effects of autonomy support and the negative effects of control. Why? This unwillingness stems in part from the misinterpretation of the meaning of autonomy from a self-determination perspective. Many theories equate autonomy with complete independence or "rugged individualism." They deem autonomous people as lacking interest in connecting with others. These theorists equate autonomy with *independence*, a term typically used to describe people who are separate, egocentric, and self-contained (Markus & Kitayama, 1991). Such a distinction is used in the concept of individualistic versus collectivistic cultures. In individualistic cultures ties between individuals are loose, whereas in collectivistic societies individuals are integrated into strong, cohesive groups (Hofstede, 1991). Each of these definitions pits autonomy against relatedness with others as if these were mutually exclusive stances. The critique of autonomy support, if viewed in this way, would be that it does not hold in collectivistic or interdependent societies in which relating to others is valued more highly than the individual. However, in self-determination theory *autonomy* refers to the experience of self-initiation or choicefulness and is not at odds with relating to others, neither is it coincident with independence.

On the contrary, autonomy and relatedness are innate, complementary needs. In asking whether one is autonomous, the issue is whether one is choicefully engaging in a practice. A person can choicefully engage in relating to others. A person can certainly be choicefully integrated into a group. However, a person can also feel forced or compelled to be part of a group and to engage in the practices associated with it. Thus, in determining how autonomous an individual is, we have to ask how choiceful or self-initiating that person feels when engaging in the group's cultural practices, regardless of whether those practices are individualistic or collectivistic in nature. When seen in this framework, autonomy is not at odds with relatedness to others. If this crucial point were understood, then the universal benefits of being autonomous—and of supporting autonomy in others—would be more easily embraced.

Another reason that people become uncomfortable in viewing control as universally problematic is that they are afraid that it will label some groups as fostering "bad" parents. This is simply not the case. Every culture includes many practices that are consistent with people's needs and some that are not. For example, in the United States there is an emphasis on extrinsic values, such as financial success, the accumulation of wealth and possessions, and appearance and a de-emphasis on the importance of relationships and community feeling. This type of valuing is at odds with people's intrinsic needs (Kasser, 2002). We argue that it is important to identify practices that are not conducive to growth and development. Controlling parenting is one of these. We advocate open discussion about how these ingrained practices might change. The truth is that no group is composed of "bad" parents. Within any culture there is so much variation that saying that parents of a culture are one way or another would be a blatant and inaccurate stereotype.

7

What Makes Parents Controlling: Pressure From Above and Below

For my family, morning is always a tricky time. Getting my two daughters off to school and my husband and me to work—all on time—is always a challenge. My elder daughter has difficulty getting organized. In my lucid moments at night when everyone is asleep, I dream up autonomy supportive strategies to help her manage herself. I will assist her as she develops a clear plan for the morning, and then I will stand back and let her deal with the consequences of being late or not following through.

In the morning, though, push comes to shove. The pressures of being late for work overwhelm me. I hear myself giving a series of commands: "Put on your shoes." "Brush your hair!" And I find myself hovering over her to make sure everything is done right. Hardly an autonomy supportive stance....

Dash (1986; cited in McLoyd & Wilson, 1991) lived for a year in one of Washington, DC's, poorest neighborhoods:

"I saw a young looking mother holding an infant in her arms and trying to keep track of two boys walking behind her. The younger boy, who looked about 3, clutched an umbrella and seemed to be having trouble with it. He was dragging its curved handle along the ground and that seemed to irritate the woman. 'Carry that umbrella right or I'll slap the [expletive] out of you,' she screamed at him. 'Carry it right, I said,' and then she slapped him in the face, knocking him off balance."

I begin this chapter with two scenarios: one involving fairly routine hassles in a middle-class home, the other the overwhelming problems that mark life in the context of poverty. They aptly illustrate how difficult it is to support children's autonomy. My thesis is that it can be tough even when one values autonomy in children and is swayed by the evidence that control undermines children's motivation and internalization. (And even when one has done some of the research herself!) Why is it that parents are controlling?

One possible reason is that parents *want* to control their children because they value the ultimate outcomes that control seems to bring: conformity and obedience. This may be true in some cases, yet there is also evidence that, for most parents, this is not the case. Several strands of evidence point in this direction.

First, although not hard-nosed evidence, two surveys of parents, one conducted by writer Alfie Kohn, and a second one conducted by me, suggest that it is not the case that most parents *ultimately* want conformity and particular outcomes for their children. Grolnick and Ryan (1989) asked a group of parents from a rural area what they would like for their children's futures. Almost every mother and father said, in essence: "I want my children to be happy doing what interests them—whatever that may be." Only 1 or 2 parents out of the 110 brought up some concrete tangible outcome such as fame or fortune. Otherwise, none of the parents mentioned getting good grades in school, making a great deal of money, or anything of that ilk.

Kohn (1998), in a survey conducted at two affluent schools, one in Texas and the other in Minnesota, asked parents what they hoped for their children. They reported that they wanted them to be happy, balanced, independent, fulfilled, productive, self-reliant, responsible, functioning, kind, thoughtful, loving, inquisitive, and confident. These adjectives clearly convey a valuing of individuality and uniqueness. Such adjectives stand in stark contrast to some of the behaviors we see on the ballfield, in the supermarket, and in our own homes when it comes to activities such as sports, doing homework, and completing chores.

Perhaps subsets of parents want to use controlling techniques. We often interpret the greater use of these techniques in poor families as the result of ignorance about parenting or different values (e.g., Piuck, 1975). However, poor parents are often aware of the fact that they are using problematic parenting strategies. They are unable to change their use of these strategies in their particular situations (Longfellow, Zelkowitz, & Saunders, 1982). Straus (1994) concluded that, with few exceptions, parents prefer not to "have to hit their children." However, 90% of parents do.

Often parents don't choose controlling techniques; rather, factors interfere with parents' abilities to provide autonomy support to their children. Some of these exist in the environments in which parents find themselves. They are stressed; they are overloaded. Others stem from the behavior of the children themselves. Still others come from one's own psychology as a parent. Thus, if we ask what makes parents controlling, we can speak of three types of pressure:

- Pressure from above
- Pressure from below
- Pressure from within

In this chapter I focus on the first two of these: pressures from above and below. In the next chapter I discuss the psychological factors, including how we become ego-involved in the performance of our children, that can lead to controlling behavior.

PRESSURE

Earlier we saw how coercion in the form of rewards, pressures to perform, and evaluation undermines children's motivation. In the same way that pressures undermine children, pressures can undermine parents' abilities to support autonomy in children. I begin with pressures surrounding the parent—those in the environment.

Pressure From Above

As Urie Bronfenbrenner (1986) argued cogently in his ecological theory, parents do not raise their children in a vacuum but are embedded in a larger context. This context may be more or less replete with resources, tangible or emotional. It may be more or less stressful on a day-to-day basis. It can also be more or less hurried and harried.

How do such stresses and pressures relate to control? These factors, including economic pressure, usurp the time and psychological availability necessary for autonomy supportive parenting. First, these pressures cause parents to focus on their own immediate predicaments. Because autonomy support entails taking the child's perspective, such a pressure is counterproductive to that task. When I am focused on beating the clock in the morning, I am hardly tuned into my daughter's struggles. When one is struggling to find the next meal, consideration of the child's eating schedule takes a back seat. Second, pressures induce one to follow the quickest and most expedient route to an outcome. In many parenting situations this may mean just going ahead and solving the problem for the child, such as telling the child what to do. In my own example it means tying my 9-year-old's shoes rather than reminding her to retie them. Allowing children to solve their own problems, rather than resolving them for them, may require more time and patience—resources that are in short supply when there is stress. Indeed, stress and other pressures can lead to irritability, which is likely to lead to angry, hostile, and controlling behavior.

What evidence is there for this in the developmental literature? Although most studies of stress or economic pressure look more generally at positive parenting, such as nurturance and responsiveness rather than the autonomy-support-to-control continuum per se, some researchers have indeed examined dimensions that are relevant to autonomy support. For example, researchers have focused on factors associated with punitiveness and harsh parenting, which would be at the controlling end of the dimension. Much of this research has looked at economic pressure, in particular, at poverty. In impoverished homes, living quarters are crowded, family members must occasionally make do without adequate basic resources, and parents are constantly tense and anxious because of their difficult circumstances. These are the ingredients that make control likely.

McLoyd and Wilson (1991) studied 92 mothers and children, all of whom were receiving Aid to Families with Dependent Children. The researchers looked at the level of economic hardship the families suffered by asking them questions such as "How difficult is it for you to meet monthly payments on your family's bills?" They also looked at parenting, on the dimension of nurturance to punitiveness, and the mother's level of psychological distress. Using a path model, they found that economic hardship was predictive of psychological distress, which was then associated with punitive parenting. A subsequent study of mothers of adolescents (McLoyd, Jayaratne, Ceballo, & Borquez, 1994) supported a similar model in which mothers who were unemployed had more depressive symptoms than those who were employed. In turn, mothers with more symptoms of depression tended to show high levels of punishment of their adolescents.

Rand Conger and his colleagues (e.g., Conger, McCarty, Yang, Lahey, & Kropp, 1984) have focused on rural families and looked at parenting behavior and the number of environmental stresses that a family experiences. These included lesser education of parents, low income, many children, and being a single parent. Conger et al. (1984) found that the greater the number of environmental stressors, the less supportive the mothers were of their children, and the more likely they were to make derogatory statements about their youngsters. They were more likely to threaten, push, or grab them. Their attitudes toward child rearing were also more controlling.

These studies (Conger et al., 1984, 1985; McLoyd et al., 1994; McLoyd & Wilson, 1991) illustrate that when parents suffer economic or other environmental stresses, they may experience depressed, anxious, and irritable moods, which then lead to harsher and more punitive parenting. Research supports the idea that stressful life situations undermine autonomy supportive parenting, although none of the studies I have discussed so far examined the control-to-autonomy-support dimension directly.

Grolnick, Weiss, McKenzie, and Wrightman (1996) looked at predictors of autonomy support versus control in parents of adolescents. Fifty-three mothers, 38 fathers, and their 13- to 18-year-old adolescents participated. Parents were interviewed separately in their homes by two researchers. The structured interview asked a set of open-ended questions for each of five areas relevant to adolescents' lives: school, friends, dating, curfews, and chores. For each area, the parent was asked how he or she motivates the child, whether he or she has any rules or expectations, and how he or she responds to positive or negative behaviors or outcomes, such as good or poor report cards. Each parent was also asked to describe the most recent conflict or disagreement he or she had with the adolescent in each area, and how that was handled.

From audiotapes of the interviews, raters scored parents on three different 5-point scales. The *values autonomy* scale concerns the extent to which the parent expresses a value for autonomy and sees its promotion as a goal, versus placing pre-eminent value on obedience and conformity. The *autonomy supportive techniques* scale assesses the degree to which parents use controlling, power-assertive, motivational, and disciplinary techniques, such as rewards and threats, versus how much they rely on more autonomy supportive methods, such as reasoning and limit setting. The third scale, *nondirectiveness*, concerns the extent to which the parent imposes his or her own agenda on the child and allows for few choices, versus including the child in decision making. These scales were averaged to form a summary autonomy support score.

Parents were also asked to complete questionnaires on stressful life events—the number of negative events that occurred in the previous 3 months, such as a death in the family, illness, repossession of the home—and the social support they had received. They also described their adolescents, but I discuss the findings for this variable in the next section.

The results showed that the more negative life events the mothers reported, the less autonomy supportive they were rated, controlling for socioeconomic status. In addition, the more negative events the family experienced, the less structure the mothers provided. There were no significant correlations between stressful events and controlling behavior in fathers. These results suggest that mothers, who are likely to be children's primary caretakers and who spend the most time with them, may be especially vulnerable to the undermining effects of stress. It is interesting that fathers who experienced more social support were rated as more involved with their adolescents. This suggests that a supportive environment for fathers helps them spend more time with their adolescents. Given that fathers may have more latitude in their roles than do mothers, their involvement may be more dependent on a supportive environment than is that of mothers.

Stress can be seen as a quality of the overall environment, or it can be evaluated on a moment-to-moment basis. Despite the quality of our overall lives, some days are worse than others. We are more rushed and more distracted at certain times. It is important to see how this affects parental control. Zussman (1980), in an interesting analogue experiment designed to mimic the "overload" state in which parents sometimes find themselves, had mothers or fathers perform distracting cognitive tasks—mental anagrams—in the presence of their two youngsters, one a toddler, the other a preschooler. In the room were toys that were difficult to operate and "attractive nuisances," such as a filled ashtray and stacks of paper. Parents and children were observed under two conditions: a low-stress situation, in which parents had no task other than to watch their children, and a high-stress condition in which they were to do the mental task as well. Zussman found that the experimental condition affected both the quality and quantity of interaction that parents had with their children. In the high-stress condition parents became less responsive and helpful toward the preschooler. Although they did not attend less to the toddler, they were more critical, restrictive, and punitive to the younger child.

These results provide some intriguing ideas about stress and parenting. Certainly one approach to dealing with stress and overload is to withdraw from the child, to be less responsive. In Zussman's (1980) study this presumably is the "strategy" used by parents with their older children, whom they probably perceived as being more capable of taking care of themselves. It is interesting that literature from the employment area suggests that, after a stressful day of work, both mothers and fathers tend to be more withdrawn from their children than following a *less* stressful day (Repetti, 1994; Repetti & Wood, 1997). However, when parents are not able to withdraw from their responsibilities—in this case, the toddler who absolutely had to be supervised—they may be more likely to use controlling parenting strategies. The use of such strategies likely undermines children's cooperation and escalates problematic child behavior, which in turn increases parents' stress levels. It is interesting that the finding that stress undermines parenting more in single-parent homes than it does in two-parent homes (Conger, Patterson, & Ge, 1995) may be due to the fact that in two-parent families the less stressed parent may "pick up the slack" for the more stressed parent. This tactic allows the overwhelmed parent to withdraw and regenerate his or her resources. Of course, a single parent is not able to rely upon that second set of hands and has to parent with whatever resources he or she can muster. This may explain the often-cited finding that single parents are more likely to use harsh discipline (Simons & Johnson, 1996) than do parents in two-parent homes.

Pressure From Below

> When Dylan was 2½, his mother began bringing him to a play group with seven other children. The moms would chat and drink coffee while the kids played in the next room. The problem was that Dylan didn't want to play. When his mother tried to shoo him into the kid's room, he would cling to her leg. If she took him into that room to show him toys or encourage him to play with the other children, she found he wouldn't let her leave. She spent every session playing with her own son. She grew embarrassed by his inability to adapt.

> One week, frustrated by not getting to talk to other mothers, she simply let him stay on her lap. Within 45 minutes, he tired of the adult conversation and wandered out to play with the children. The following week she again allowed him to sit on her lap. Within 30 minutes he joined the kids. The next week it took even less time.

> "I should have realized that Dylan's temperament at that stage was that he was a slow-to-warm child," his mother said years later. "But now, my goodness, he's about the most social kid you could find. It just took time for him to find his own way and grow out of that stage. Had I not pushed him off my lap so strenuously, he would have gone off to play with the kids in three weeks instead of twenty. I should have taken my cues from him."

Since Richard Bell's pioneering work in the 1960s (e.g., 1968), we have come to accept that parents not only affect their children but also that children affect their parents. This is certainly likely to be the case with control. Children who are cooperative, who do their work or their chores, and who don't talk back may be the recipients of more autonomy support. Those who are uncooperative, who test their parents' patience, and who don't take responsibility for their work may elicit more control. It is likely to be easier to involve children in decisions, and to take their viewpoint, if the children are agreeable and tend to comply easily. Furthermore, children who competently pursue their work or studies may be less likely to elicit control than do those who are needier.

If we wish to study how children's behaviors affect parents, we run into the bidirectional effects problem. We have already seen that autonomy supportive parenting facilitates children's competence and positive behavior, but how are we to tell whether relations between negative behavior and control represent child-to-parent effects, or parent-to-child effects? Several strategies have been used to deal with this problem. One strategy is to identify characteristics that are relatively stable and likely to be inherited, such as temperament, and then to relate those to parenting. With this strategy one can look at relations between temperamental characteristics and parenting as they unfold over time. A second technique is to observe mothers interacting with other parents' children to ascertain whether particular children elicit control across caregivers. Finally, behavioral genetics researchers have attempted to determine how genetic characteristics of children result in different levels of control in the parenting environment.

Temperament. In identifying characteristics of children that affect parenting it would be optimal to find characteristics that are innate and uninfluenced by the environment. Of course, such characteristics do not exist, as even in utero the environment is influencing the child. Children's dispositions and behaviors are always a complex function of what they bring and of their experiences. However, researchers have identified certain temperamental characteristics that are *relatively* stable and likely to be heritable. Nonetheless, most researchers acknowledge that temperamental characteristics are changeable. Every parent knows that children are born with personalities and tendencies that differ even within families. Some children are shy, others are more outgoing, some are easily distressed or upset. Then there are children who are less easily riled and, of course there are children who are highly active and those who are very sedentary (Buss & Plomin, 1984). Thomas, Chess, and Birch (1968) described one set of temperamental features labeled *difficulty*, in which they portrayed a baby who is often in a negative mood, shows high-intensity reactions, who withdraws from new stimuli, and is slow to adapt to new situations. The *easy* baby, on the other hand, generally has a positive mood, regular body functions, and a positive approach to new situations. What evidence is there that such characteristics are associated with levels of control?

Correlational studies support the connection between child difficulty and parental control. Rutter and Quinton (1984), in their 4-year longitudinal study of children of mentally ill parents, showed that children who have adverse temperamental features—a composite of low regularity, low malleability, negative mood, and low fastidiousness—were more likely than other children to be targets of parental hostility, criticism, and irritability.

Further evidence comes from research with infants. Bates (1980) found that at ages 6 and 13 months there were few relations between infant difficulty and mother behavior. By 24 months, however, there was more conflict between mothers and children, who were described as difficult. Mothers of these more difficult 2-year-olds were more likely to use power assertion, including frequent control efforts, frequent repetitions, prohibitions, and more frequent taking away of objects. D. M. Buss (1981) showed that power struggles were more frequent between children and mothers and fathers when children were more active. Lee and Bates (1985) found that toddlers with difficult temperaments were more resistant to maternal attempts to exert authority and that their negative behavior was more likely to be met with coercive responses by mothers. Finally, on the opposite end of the spectrum, children's fearfulness—as reported by mothers and observed in unfamiliar laboratory situations—was positively associated with the use of gentle discipline that deemphasized power assertion, as observed in both the laboratory and at home (Kochanska, 1995).

In our own adolescent project (Grolnick, Weiss, McKenzie, & Wrightman, 1996) we took the perspective that the way parents experience and label a child's behavior will be most proximally related to their parenting. We thus asked mothers and fathers about the "difficulty" of their adolescents. For example, we asked parents to rate items such as "My child is even-tempered and not moody" on a scale that ranged from *very true* to *not true at all*. We also inquired about parents' view of adolescence—whether they believe that adolescence is a difficult stage. For example, we asked parents to rate the validity of the statement "Adolescence is a difficult time of life for children and their parents." We were interested in whether the way in which parents experienced their adolescents and the way they viewed the period of adolescence would be associated with how involved they were with their adolescents and whether they tended to treat the child in a more autonomy supportive versus more controlling manner.

First, the results for parents' perceptions of their own adolescents indicated that mothers who believed their teenagers were more difficult were more controlling than mothers who rated their adolescents as easier. Thus, mothers may be tailoring their levels of control to characteristics of their children. It is interesting that this relation did not hold true for fathers. Rather, for them, there was a significant relation between difficulty and involvement. This suggests that when fathers felt their children were more difficult, they were likely to withdraw from interaction rather than controlling the adolescents. This may be because, although fathers have become more involved with their children over time (Silverstein, 2002), they still have more latitude than mothers do in how involved they are. In other words, mothers may not have the option of extracting themselves from parenting situations. As a consequence, they may end up responding to difficult behaviors with control rather than withdrawal.

The results for parents' views of the general period of adolescence indicate that fathers who see that time as difficult are more controlling. This does not hold true for mothers. The results also indicate that fathers are more influenced by their stereotypes of adolescents than are mothers. Perhaps this is a function of fathers' lesser experience with teenagers; they spend markedly less time with them relative to mothers (Montemayor, 1982).

In this same study (Grolnick, Weiss, McKenzie, & Wrightman, 1996), we wondered whether there would be transactions between the environment in which parents parented and the characteristics of the adolescents. More specifically, we wondered whether in nonstressful environments parents would tailor their parenting to qualities of their adolescents. In less conducive environments parents would be less likely to do so. To examine this question we divided families into those who were high or low in stress, social support, or marital satisfaction. Next, we computed correlations between child difficulty and parenting within the high and low groups. We conducted these analyses for mothers only, because the number of fathers was small. The results indicated links between difficulty of adolescents and parenting in the conducive contexts but not the nonconducive contexts. More specifically, in low-stress and supportive environments parents of more difficult adolescents provided more control than did parents of less difficult adolescents. However, in the high-stress environments levels of control were not linked to characteristics of the adolescents. Parents are more likely to tailor their parenting characteristics to the adolescents within supportive environments than in nonsupportive environments. This demonstrates how difficult contexts can make parents control—regardless of whether the child "pulls" for control. Parents know this is true. On easy days, it is only the extreme behaviors of one's children that lead one to push, coerce, and yell. On difficult days, even a small disagreement can set a parent off.

Of course, all of these studies are correlational in nature. When researchers correlate two variables—for example, parental control and children's difficulty—they cannot determine why the two are related. They cannot tell if the difficulty causes the control, if the control causes the difficulty, if each contributes to the other, or if the two are not causally related at all. Although parents who have difficult children may respond with more control, it is also plausible that parents who are more controlling increase children's reactance. Reactance involves people attempting to restore their freedom by acting against a control, such as by refusing to comply, engaging in negative behaviors, or complying but subtly sabotaging the situation (Brehm, 1966). More controlling parents may actually *create* more difficulty in their children. When my colleagues and I see children and parents in our studies, we catch them in cycles of parent-to-child and child-to-parent influence. Careful, moment-to-moment analyses of parent–child interaction show that oppositional behavior leads to irritability, which evokes control, which sustains noncompliance (Patterson, 1982).

Consider this example. Notice how each coercive, controlling gesture is met by further coercion in a vicious upward spiral.

1. Sally teases her older brother, Sam. To make her stop, he yells at her.
2. A few minutes later, Sally calls her brother a nasty name. Sam then gives chase. He hits her.
3. Sally stops calling him names. Whimpering, she hits him back. He withdraws. Then he approaches her and hits her again. The conflict escalates.
4. At this point, the mother intervenes. However, her children are too emotionally distraught to listen to reason, so she finds herself applying punitive and coercive tactics to make them stop their battle.
5. The fighting does stop. However, the children now begin to whine, cry, and yell at their mother. She backs off. The next time the children antagonize each other and become involved in an unbearable conflict, the mother is likely to use even more coercion to get them to stop. The children again apply their own methods of counter-coercion to induce her to "lay off." The family atmosphere becomes increasingly unpleasant for everyone.

Gerald Patterson, a psychologist who has spent many years doing research and clinical work with families caught in coercive cycles, suggests that to break families out of this coercive cycle one must work with all the members of the family in order to teach them new approaches to dealing with problems. For example, rather than meeting coercion with more coercion, he suggests time out for coercive behaviors. Patterson (1982) showed amazing success using this program with troubled families in his Oregon clinic.

Other Parents' Children.   Although it is significant that parents' experiences of their adolescents are predictive of control, one way to get around the *theoretical* problem of bidirectional influences is to manipulate the "difficultness" of children in experiments. Beth Jelsma (1982) did just that in a study in which she gave mothers the task of teaching anagrams to other people's 9- to 11-year-olds. Each mother taught one child. These children were actually confederates. Half were trained to be difficult, uncooperative, and disinterested, and half were asked to be easy, cooperative, and engaged. Tapes of the interactions showed that mothers were more controlling with the more difficult children.

K. E. Anderson, Lytton, and Romney (1986) had mothers of normal children and mothers of conduct-disordered children interact in the laboratory with their own or with others' children. More negative responses were made to the conduct-disordered children, whether they were the mother's own or someone else's child. In addition, mothers showed fewer positive behaviors toward their own children, regardless of whether they were conduct-disordered. This study provides further support that control is at least in part driven by child behavior.

Behavioral Genetics.   We saw earlier that parents, whether with their own or with others' children, provide levels of controllingness that are, at least in part, a result of characteristics of the children with whom they interact. What about children in the same family? Do parents provide similar levels of control across children, or is each child provided with different levels, because each one has unique characteristics? Furthermore, if each child is treated differently, are these differences the result of something in the child's genes? If so, this would provide strong evidence for child-to-parent effects.

A preliminary issue in addressing questions about genetic effects on parental control is: Does each child in a family receive similar levels of control? To address this issue, Robert Plomin and his colleagues (Plomin, Reiss, Hetherington, & Howe, 1994) had siblings within the same families rate how much negative control—coercion and punitiveness—their mothers and fathers provided them. The researchers then correlated siblings' ratings. The correlations for parental control ratings of the two siblings were .36 for mothers and .28 for fathers. This indicates that siblings were reporting only moderately similar levels of control from the same parent. Although parents' self-ratings of the control they provided to their children were higher—.63 and .69 for mothers and fathers, respectively—there was still a great deal of variance in control that was not accounted for by having the same parent. Of course, there can be many reasons for the lack of consistency in how siblings are treated. For example, children within the same family may actually be treated differently, or children may receive similar treatment but, because of their own characteristics, they interpret this behavior differently (McCartney, Robeson, Jordan, & Mouradian, 1991). In either case, the net effect is that children in the same family definitely experience different levels of control.

Behavioral geneticists seek greater understanding of the origins of these child-to-parent effects. They ask: How much of the person–environment correlation—say, uncooperative children receiving more control—is genetically influenced? In other words, is the reason children are exposed to more or less control because of some genetic characteristics they bring into the world? In relation to parental control, two strategies have been adopted to test this question: First, one can see whether the relation between levels of control that children experience within the same family are more similar for children who have greater genetic similarity, for example, twins versus siblings and full siblings versus half-siblings. If children who are genetically more similar receive more consistent levels of control than do those who share fewer genes, then the genes could be said to account for the way in which children are treated. These children live in the same home, after all. In fact, Plomin et al. (1994) demonstrated that the more genetically similar children in the same families were, the closer were their reports of both mother's and father's levels of control. This certainly supports the idea that the level of control in children's family environments is at least partially due to genetic factors.

A second approach researchers take is to study children adopted at birth. This strategy can determine whether adoptive parents administer more control to children who are at risk for problematic behavior because of their biological parents' characteristics. If this is the case, then we know that some genetically based characteristics in children contribute to levels of parental control. Xiaojia Ge and his colleagues (Ge, Conger, & Stewart, 1996) used this strategy to show that adoptive parents displayed more harsh parenting toward adopted adolescents whose biological parents were diagnosed with an antisocial disorder or who were alcoholic than they did toward teenagers whose biological parents did not have these problems. O'Connor, Deater-Deckard, Fulker, Rutter, and Plomin (1998) divided children into high and low genetic risk for antisocial behavior on the basis of their biological mothers' history of antisocial behavior. They then had adoptive parents rate the level of negative control they provided to the children. Adoptive parents of children at genetic risk reported using more negative control than did adoptive parents of children who were not at risk. Furthermore, the effects of risk status were mediated by the externalizing behavior of the children. The ones who were at genetic risk exhibited more problematic behavior. These troublesome actions led parents to use more control.

Does the above-described research mean that parental control is a done deal? Are parents destined to provide high control to children who are unlucky enough to possess genes that pull for it? Are children and parents hopelessly trapped in aversive cycles in which defiance leads to control—which leads to more defiance? The answer to these questions is an unequivocal no. Modern views of genes emphasize that genes provide propensities but do not determine behavior. They only increase the chance of x or y happening, given that all other factors are equal, which, of course, they are not. Our brains are separate from genes, and thus choice can override. The effects of genes can be overcome by many influences. A case in point is Patterson's (1982) successful interventions, mentioned earlier, for decreasing levels of coercive interaction between parents and children.

Child Competence and Control: An Example of How Well-Meaning Behavior Backfires.   Another issue, related to but also separate from difficulty, is child competence. There is strong evidence that the more competent children are, the more autonomy support and the less control they receive. The case of child competence is different from that of antisocial or problem behavior. In the case of acting out and other overactive sorts of behavior, which have been the subject of many of the genetic and experimental studies, one may argue that a parent *has* to provide increased control (although I take issue with this notion) because, after all, you can't tolerate these behaviors. The reasoning for the excess control provided to poorly achieving and less competent children is more likely to be that these children *need* more control. This is a more direct illustration of how well-meaning parenting backfires.

In a recent study in my laboratory (Grolnick, Gurland, DeCourcey, & Jacob, 2002), which I will describe in greater detail in the next chapter, we observed mothers and their third-grade children working on homework-like tasks together. Mothers' behavior was rated on the continuum of autonomy support to control. We also obtained children's report card grades in reading and math. Grades were one of the most powerful predictors of mothers' control: Mothers of children who did more poorly in school directed their children more in the laboratory task, took over more of the task, solved more of the problems themselves, and were rated as more controlling overall.

One explanation for the correlation between children's grades and mothers' level of control is that the children who had poorer grades in school were having more trouble with our task, hence they needed increased levels of control. However, our coding system took into account the child's need for intervention. If the child was having difficulty, and the parent intervened, the parent was not coded as controlling. We reserved controlling codes for instances in which the parent directed or channeled the child's behavior beyond what the child required. We could therefore determine that the controlling mothers of poorer students controlled their children beyond what their *immediate* behavior would warrant. One parent in our study, for example, alerted us at the start of the task that her child was not good at homework and would have trouble with it. She proceeded to direct and control the child's behavior before he displayed any difficulties at all. In fact, through her control, she contributed to his lack of understanding of and engagement with the task. Such controlling behavior may create a self-fulfilling prophecy, linking control and incompetence. Of course, as we saw earlier, controlling behavior may have also contributed to the low levels of competence children displayed from the outset. In any case, it is clear that children with a history of difficulty in school evoke more controlling behavior than is warranted given their own current behavior.

Similarly, Pomerantz and Eaton (2001) found that mothers of children who received poor grades in school were more likely to endorse and use control than were mothers of children doing well academically. It is interesting that the authors obtained both pre- and postmeasure grades and found that children's premeasure grades were most associated with control, suggesting that children's grades may lead parents to engage in controlling behaviors.

The ways in which low competence elicits control are also evident in the literature on special populations. Grolnick and Ryan (1990) had teachers rate the amount of control, including prodding and pushing, afforded to children who were learning disabled or low achievers and compared these ratings with those for a randomly selected group of normally achieving children. Teachers reported using more control with the learning-disabled children than they did with the other groups. When we polled the children themselves, the learning-disabled and low-achieving children reported lower perceived competence and lower motivation than did the normally achieving children. Learning-disabled children were more likely than the other groups to say that their achievement outcomes were in the hands of powerful others—notably, the teacher—rather than in their own hands. The added control for these children may translate into feelings of not being in charge and of incompetence (Pomerantz & Eaton, 2000). Those perceptions then feed into further motivational deficits.

Perhaps this is natural. After all, parents and teachers just want to give more to their children who need it the most. Do less competent children simply *need* more control? That's unlikely.

As we saw earlier, control undermines motivation and learning. Increasing levels of control with children who have a history of poor performance is likely to decrease a sense of autonomy, which further undermines motivation. Children with special needs undoubtedly require more patience and resources from their teachers and parents. They may also require more involvement or structure because they do not have the capacity to organize their own behaviors. However, increased control is only likely to undermine their motivation even further, and their motivation is already at risk because of prolonged experiences of failure. The use of enhanced controls, whether in the form of contingency programs or more directive parenting or teaching methods, is sometimes the result of frustration or fear that children will be left behind. Or it comes from a paucity of alternative strategies. I suggest that controlling strategies should not become the method of choice. When behavior is out of control, and some control, whether self-determined or not, is the proximal goal, then certainly it may be imperative to implement quick methods to gain control, such as reward programs or directives. The point is that these methods should be used only sparingly and as short-term, interim ways of controlling behavior. These controlling methods can never serve as long-term strategies to facilitate internal motivation and regulation. In fact, they work against the ultimate goal of having *all* children experience a sense of self-determination in their lives.

Another Example: Children Diagnosed With Attention Deficit Hyperactivity Disorder. Another case in point is the child diagnosed with attention deficit hyperactivity disorder (ADHD). ADHD is a chronic condition occurring in approximately 5% of school-age children (American Psychiatric Association, 1987). It is characterized by symptoms of inattention, hyperactivity, and impulsivity. This disorder clearly has effects on both children's behavior toward parents and parents' behavior toward their children. Children diagnosed with ADHD are less likely to comply with their parents' requests, more likely to be negative, and sustain compliance for a shorter time than nondiagnosed children. It is not surprising that parents of ADHD children were found to be more directive and commanding and more negative toward their children than a group of control parents (Barkley, 1985). Johnston (1996) referred to this pattern as a *negative-reactive response* in which parents react to their children's problematic behavior with negative and controlling behaviors. Consistent with earlier arguments, I suggest that the most likely explanation of this pattern is a reciprocal one in which child difficulty and noncompliance are met with increasing levels of control that further noncompliance.

Perhaps high levels of control are an inevitable response to ADHD behavior, and perhaps this is even optimal. Research has shown that, although understandable, it is neither inevitable nor optimal. For example, taking into account children's behavior during an interaction (that might explain parents' reactions), parents who were more negative during the interaction had ADHD boys who were more noncompliant in the classroom and on the playground than sons of parents who were more positive in the interactions (C. A. Anderson, Hinshaw, & Simmel, 1994). More negative and controlling interactions appear to worsen ADHD children's behavior over time. Furthermore, even though parents of children with ADHD are on average more controlling than those of nondiagnosed children, there is a range of behaviors and attitudes in parents of ADHD children, and these attitudes and behaviors make a difference. For example, diagnosed children of mothers who held more authoritative attitudes (i.e., valued autonomy yet believed in firm enforcement of rules) were more accepted by their peers than children whose mothers held less authoritative attitudes (Hinshaw, Zupan, Simmel, Nigg, & Melnick, 1997). The message here is that, although control is an understandable response to the types of behaviors exhibited by children diagnosed with ADHD, if parents can maintain structure in an autonomy supportive manner they can help to promote their children's social competence. This clearly is a difficult task, but a worthwhile one.

CONCLUSION

There are clearly many factors in parents' environments and in children themselves that increase the likelihood of parental control. The stresses under which parents function on a day-to-day basis make it difficult to maintain an autonomy supportive stance with children, even when parents value and emulate such a stance. Children's own behavior certainly evokes controlling responses. It is easy to see how many families are caught in coercive cycles of control and negativity. It is up to parents, and the communities around them, to create contexts in which autonomy support is possible and in which alternative strategies for facilitating child competence and well-being are available.

8

What Makes Parents Controlling: Pressure From Within

At one of my daughters' recent swim meets I sat next to a mother of a child from the other team. She chatted with me and other parents about her son's swimming times. At one point, she said "We decided we would swim this year." I found her emphasis on "we" quite curious. At that moment her son came over, obviously upset. "I'm not going to swim," he announced. His mother struggled for a minute to gain her composure. She glanced around to see if anyone was watching. Then she looked him straight in the eye and, with desperation, said "We came all the way here, and you are going to swim." He shook his head. She countered his refusal with a further attempt at persuasion: "If you don't swim today, it's over. You are not going to do this to me again." Tears filled his eyes, and his thin shoulders shook as he sobbed in silence.

In watching a tape of a mother and her third-grader in one of my studies, I am struck with the mother's obvious desire to allow her child to lead while remaining responsive. As the two write a poem together, the child becomes obviously stuck. The mother offers hints, but they do not help. I see the woman reach out to take hold of the pencil, then pull her hand back. This aborted movement happens several times. Finally, in a moment of frustration, she grabs the pencil and finishes the poem. There is no look of satisfaction on either the daughter's or the mother's face at the end of the task.

Although external pressure, a child's own personality characteristics, or both, may lead parents to become more or less controlling, there are also psychological processes within parents that lead them to be controlling. These processes can either function in conjunction with outside forces or separate from them. Parents are not neutral in regard to their children's behavior. Whether for good or for bad, parents and children are intertwined in ways that can transform children's performance into parents' performance, children's triumphs into parents' triumphs, children's defeats into parents' failures.

A particular challenge of mine in the last few years has been to understand how parents can sometimes become "hooked" into focusing on their children's performance. Part of my reason for becoming interested in this issue is my own experience with my two daughters. Although I strongly believe in supporting children's autonomy—and had planned to always do so—I realize that it is surprisingly difficult to keep my own ego out of their activities. I find myself, for example, paying a bit too much attention to my daughter's times at her swim meets (and wanting to know what times the other children got). We sometimes fall into battles about making homework neat, as if the homework were mine and not hers. I discover that I am more concerned about my children having friends and being popular than I thought I would be. I worry that my daughters may not be the most sought after of their peers.

When their report cards arrive, I focus on their grades more than I imagined I would. When I speak to the teacher on open-school night, I scrutinize her every sentence for subtle hints as to how my child is really doing. I struggle with choices about activities. Should I let my daughters hang around at home after school, or should I make sure that they are engaging in extracurricular activities that are "good for them"? I know what I think is right, as I am a great believer in the importance of free time and space for creative development, but I am nagged by worries that my children might miss out on something that other children are getting.

Sometimes the issues of concern or internal pressure I feel are just that—clenched fists and high blood pressure at swim meets or on the soccer field. I am relieved to say I have seldom taken action. Whether or not I act, though, these are surprisingly intense feelings. What is this all about? There are no visible pressures leading me to my emotions, yet I clearly become hooked into my children's performance in ways that I do not feel are consistent with my philosophy. In this chapter I explore the process of getting hooked, or ego involved, in children's performance, and I provide some explanations about why parents are so vulnerable.

THE CLINICAL VIEW

Until now, there have been few models for understanding the psychology of parental control. The prevailing view has been the clinical one, which focuses not on the psychology per se but on the psychopathology of control. The clinical literature has provided at least two models. Both of them are pathological, and both may be true for some families.

First, object-relations theorists, such as Alice Miller and Margaret Mahler, have suggested that some parents, damaged by their own upbringings, have difficulty separating their own needs from those of their children. These parents have a hard time seeing life from their children's perspectives and acting in ways that are in the children's best interests. Miller's often-quoted book, *The Drama of the Gifted Child* (1981), portrays a narcissistic mother who uses her child to fulfill her own egoistic needs. The mother cannot see the child for who she is, because the child is not a person in her own right but rather a self-object or extension of the parent. Insecure herself, the narcissistic parent requires the child to act in specific ways, fulfilling her own unfulfilled hopes, wishes, and desires to retain her self-esteem and equilibrium. When the child pursues her own interests, this parent accuses her of being inconsiderate or "bad." The child in turn does what is expected and valued by her parents and loses her own sense of what interests her and what she loves. In this model, the controlling parent does not have the psychological resources to act in another way. The processes of empathy and perspective taking are so impaired that only long-term therapy can make a difference in parenting.

Another model for understanding control, which comes out of the family therapy literature, is the enmeshed family. Salvador Minuchin's model, developed at the Philadelphia Child Guidance Center, focuses on the enmeshed family as lacking boundaries between individuals or subsets of individuals. Boundaries are invisible enclosures surrounding parts of the family (e.g., individuals, the couple, the parents and children, etc.). When boundaries are too strong or rigid, family members lack a sense of contact and sharing with each other. Parents may not know what is going on with their children, or they may not have the emotional closeness or ties to confide in one other or to take on each other's causes. In the opposite situation, the enmeshed family, the boundaries between family members are too porous. In these families, individuals are not allowed to be separate people. Parents may too readily feel their children's feelings for them and not allow them to have their own lives and experiences. Differences among family members are not well tolerated. In such families, parents intrude into children's lives and feelings and are unable to see children for who they are (Minuchin, 1974). Individuals must sell out their own individuality to be part of the group.

These pathological models for understanding controlling parents are certainly reasonable for a subset of parents. However, another model is needed to understand how relatively healthy parents, even those who may value autonomy in their children and believe autonomy supportive parenting works, may sometimes behave in a controlling manner.

THE DYNAMICS OF INTERNAL PRESSURE

Contrasted with the external pressures from the environment and the challenges of parenting difficult or poorly performing children are the internal pressures parents experience to have their children perform: to do well in school, to be the star soccer player, to look the best. Internal pressures can be just as intense and compelling as those that come from without.

One of the concepts that has been linked to internal pressure is *ego involvement* (Sherif & Cantril, 1947). When people are ego involved, their performance has ramifications for their own self-esteem. In other words, their self-esteem hinges on their performance. People will feel good about themselves, and be proud if they perform well, but they will feel bad about themselves, embarrassed and perhaps ashamed if they perform poorly. Thus performance poses a threat to self-esteem. People are highly motivated to protect their self-esteem by ensuring positive outcomes. By contrast, when people are engaged in the tasks themselves, they take part in them out of interest rather than the desire to display positive performance.

Richard Ryan (1982) linked the concept of ego involvement with internal control, suggesting that when people hinge their self-esteem on their performance they experience a push or pressure to perform that comes from within. They pressure and evaluate themselves, much as others might evaluate them. For example, in writing this book, I may be involved in two different ways. First, I can write it because the task is enjoyable or because I feel that what I have to say is important and I want to get the word out. As I compose my words, I focus my attention on the process of writing. On the other hand, I can give the book surplus meaning and have something more on the line than the book itself. I could be focused on the outcome, whether the book will be well reviewed, whether it will be adopted for courses, whether people will like it. I could hinge my own feelings about myself as a writer, a psychologist, even as a person, on the book. If the book does well, I will feel proud and worthy. However, if it fails, if no one understands it, if my colleagues malign it, I will feel unworthy, useless, a failure. In this case, my experience will be one of feeling pressured to do it right and worrying whether it is good enough. My attention will be focused less on the writing itself and more on myself and my imagined audience. I will experience pressure and tension from within because the book has meaning beyond the moment.

Consistent with this idea, a number of studies have shown that the state of ego involvement, with its accompanying internal stress and pressure, is undermining of intrinsic motivation (e.g., Plant & Ryan, 1985; Ryan, 1982), much like external pressures such as rewards and evaluation. For example, Ryan (1982) had college students solve hidden-picture puzzles in either ego-involved or task-involved conditions. In the ego-involved condition he led students to believe that how they did on the task was related to their IQs (something obviously of great significance to students). In the task-involved condition no such link was made. He showed that the ego-involving manipulation resulted in greater feelings of pressure and tension than task involvement as well as lower intrinsic motivation to pursue the tasks in a free-choice session.

In Ryan's (1982) study participants became ego involved when their own performance had ramifications outside of the task itself, that is, when their own performance had the potential to make them feel that they would be seen as "smart" or "dumb." However, there are a variety of instances in which people's feelings hinge not on their own performance but on the performance of another person. For instance, how a student fares on a test might alter how the teacher assesses her teaching. How a child dresses might affect how the mother feels she will be judged as a parent. In these examples, teachers and parents become ego involved in children's performance, behavior, or outcomes, and this ego involvement is likely to influence the way teachers and parents interact with children.

Deci et al. (1982) examined a related phenomenon in an analogue study of teachers. College students were told that they would be "teaching" other students to solve puzzles. These "teachers" were given one of two orientations to their task: one emphasizing performance standards (what the authors called the *controlling* induction) and the other with no specific performance requirements (the *informational* induction). The teachers then taught other college students to solve the puzzles. It was presumed that teachers who thought they were responsible for students performing up to standards would feel that they were not good teachers if their students did not perform well. Thus, they would be invested (i.e., ego involved) in the students' performance for their own views of themselves. Conversely, participants who were led to believe that there were no specific performance requirements would not feel that their worth as teachers was linked to their students' performance.

Teaching sessions were audiotaped and later coded (Deci et al., 1982). Teachers who received the controlling induction were judged to be more demanding and controlling. They talked more, let students work alone less, used three times as many directives and should-type statements, and they used 2½ times more criticisms than teachers in the informational condition. Students with teachers in the controlling condition solved more puzzles with the help of the teacher but fewer puzzles alone. Thus, when teachers are pressured and led to believe students' performance has meaning for them, they become more controlling.

There are other interesting results from Deci et al.'s (1982) study. First, ratings made by teachers after the sessions showed that teachers in the controlling condition liked their students more than did the teachers in the informational condition, presumably because the students in the controlling group "performed" for the teachers. Thus, the use of control did not produce a negative response toward the students. Second, there were no differences in reported enjoyment, effectiveness, rated interest in the puzzles, or willingness to take part in similar studies, between teachers in the two conditions. Thus, the state of having performance standards did not appear to be especially unpleasant to these teachers. I return to this point later.

Winch and Grolnick (1993) used another kind of analogue, that of a counseling situation. A set of students (the "counselees") were given unsolvable anagrams to work on prior to talking with a "counselor." College student "counselors" were then given the task of interacting with a "counselee" to find out what his or her experience had been with the anagrams. Half the counselors were assigned to the ego-involved condition; they were told that the session was a "test of how good they were at interacting with another person" and that such a skill would have implications for other important life tasks. The other half of the counselors were in the task-involved condition and were told that the experimenters were interested in how people disclosed information about their experiences.

Interactions between counselors and counselees were audiotaped and later coded. The ego-involved counselors were judged to be more controlling than the task-involved counselors; however, although the ego-involved counselors rated themselves as more pressured and anxious immediately after receiving the ego-involving manipulation, they did not rate themselves as more pressured or anxious or as enjoying themselves less during the interaction.

So what about parents interacting with their children? Will parents who are ego involved in their children's performance show more control? What impact will this have on their children? Grolnick, Gurland, DeCourcey, and Jacob (2002) examined this issue in a study that was part of a series on parent involvement.

In this study (Grolnick et al., 2002), parents and their third-grade children completed school-like tasks together in our laboratory. Half of the parent–child dyads worked together under a condition that we thought would result in parents being ego involved in their children's performance on the tasks. In this condition (called the *high-pressure* condition), we focused the parents on the evaluation of their children by stressing to the parents that the children would be tested on the task, by mentioning that there was a set of standards that the child had to meet and by suggesting that the parents were responsible for how the children performed ("ensure your child performs well enough"). Parents who were not ego involved (in the low-pressure condition) had no performance standards to meet, and the instructions de-emphasized parental responsibility for children's performance.

Sixty mothers and their third-grade children participated in the study, conducted at our Child and Family Development Laboratory at Clark University. On arriving, mothers rated their attitudes toward child rearing on a scale that ranged from *supporting autonomy* to *controlling children's behavior*. Children rated their mothers' autonomy support at home and completed questionnaires about their own motivational qualities. Each mother–child dyad then completed two homework-like tasks, similar to those that a third-grader might bring home from school. One was a map task that required them to give directions to different locations on a large map. The second was a poem task that required them to label rhyming patterns of poems and then write a quatrain (four-lined poem with a particular pattern), which is what the mother and child were doing in the example at the beginning of this chapter.

The order of the two tasks was counterbalanced. Each mother was assigned to either the high-pressure condition or the low-pressure condition. In the high-pressure condition the mother was told: "Your role is to ensure that your child learns to give directions [write a poem]. We will be testing him/her afterwards to make sure that he/she performs well enough." In the low-pressure condition the mother was told: "Your role is to help your child learn how to give directions [write a poem]. We will be asking him/her some questions afterwards but there is no particular level at which he/she needs to perform."

After the experimental induction, mothers filled out an affect rating scale, and then mothers and children worked on the tasks. Next, mothers and children separately completed questionnaires about their experience, including their feelings of competence, enjoyment, pressure and tension, and effort expended. Finally, mothers left the room, and children were given a new task of the same type to solve on their own (again, giving directions or writing a quatrain). This task was included to determine whether children's internalization of what they had learned differed as a function of the condition under which the dyad had worked.

Videotapes of the mothers and children working on the tasks were coded by two raters, both for types of statements the mothers made to their children— whether they were controlling or autonomy supportive—and for the types of behaviors they used in working with the children. The controlling and autonomy supportive codings are laid out in Figure 8.1. Controlling statements included directives (such as "Do that one now"), taking over (reading the items instead of allowing the child to do so), and telling the answers. Autonomy supportive statements included giving information or strategies when the child needed them ("That street is too far. Try one closer") and providing feedback ("You're almost there!"). Controlling behaviors included leading (pointing to the part to come next), taking over (pulling the map from the child), and showing the child the answer. Autonomy supportive behaviors included being available to provide assistance, pointing out information when the child was stuck, and providing nonverbal feedback (e.g., nodding one's head). In addition, for each 5-sec interval mothers were given an overall rating for how autonomy supportive versus controlling their behaviors and vocalizations were. The performance of the mother and child dyad on the map and poem tasks, as well as how the child performed when his or her mother was not available to assist, were coded. We also had two coders rate the creativity of the poem the child wrote alone.

Grolnick et al. (2002) expected that mothers in the high-pressure condition would use more controlling verbal and nonverbal behaviors and be rated as more controlling than those in the low-pressure condition. We also expected that mothers who came into the session with more controlling attitudes would be more controlling in the session. We also wondered if mothers who were more or less controlling at the start of the mother–child interaction would be differently affected by the condition under which they worked. In other words, one of the research questions was whether all mothers would be equally affected by being focused on their children's performance or whether some would be affected more than others.

Content Coding of Mother Vocalizations and Behaviors

Verbal	**Nonverbal**
Controlling	Controlling
• Directives	• Leading behavior
• Taking over	• Taking over
• Giving answers	• Giving answers
Autonomy Supportive	Autonomy Supportive
• Feedback	• Information
• Information	• Available

FIG. 8.1. Content codings of mothers' vocalizations and behaviors.

The results for the poem task showed that the condition under which mothers worked had a big effect on their behavior (Grolnick et al., 2002). Specifically, mothers in the high-pressure condition used more directives, showed somewhat more taking-over behavior, and were rated as more controlling overall than those in the low-pressure condition. Figure 8.2 depicts this effect for the overall rating of autonomy support. In addition, mothers who held controlling attitudes to begin with used more controlling statements and behaviors with their children (e.g., more taking over, somewhat more directives, more leading) and were less available to help their children when the children needed assistance. They were also rated as more controlling overall.

Thus, for Grolnick et al.'s (2002) poem task, when mothers worked under pressure to have their children perform, they were more controlling verbally with their children. It is interesting that the strongest effects on this verbal task were for verbal behavior. However, mothers' behaviors were also highly dependent on the styles that they brought into the laboratory. This is not surprising, because mothers and children have a history of working together and are likely to have established ways of interacting, especially on tasks similar to those they routinely do at home.

The results for the map task were a bit different. On this nonverbal task there were more effects of the intervention on nonverbal behavior, but this time we found that, although there were some effects of condition alone, some mothers

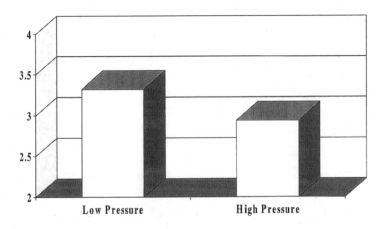

FIG. 8.2.   Mean verbal autonomy support: Poem task.

were affected by the condition more than others. Mothers in the high-pressure condition took over more, and they indicated the answers to their children more frequently than did mothers in the low-pressure condition. As in the poem task, the attitudes mothers held toward autonomy support were highly predictive of their behavior; mothers whose children rated them as more autonomy supportive at home used fewer controlling verbal and nonverbal behaviors and were rated as more autonomy supportive in the laboratory. Grolnick et al. (2002) also found that the effects of the condition in which parents worked were particularly striking for one group: the mothers who came in with controlling styles. In fact, the results showed that mothers with highly autonomy supportive styles were relatively unaffected by the condition and, in some cases, they were even more autonomy supportive during the task than were highly autonomy supportive mothers in the low-pressure condition. This interaction effect is depicted in Figure 8.3 where controlling mothers in the high pressure condition used the highest levels of controlling behavior. Thus, mothers who had controlling styles and were subjected to the evaluation of the high-pressure condition were highly controlling. The other three groups were quite similar in their behavior.

Another set of Grolnick et al.'s (2002) analyses looked at whether the condition under which mothers worked and mothers' styles when they came into the laboratory had effects on how the dyad performed on the tasks and, in particu-

Nonverbal Control Composite: Map Task

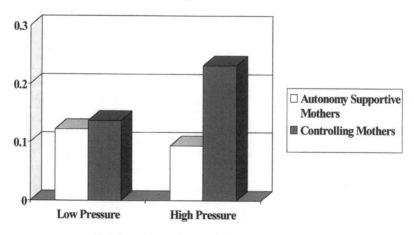

FIG. 8.3. Nonverbal control composite: Map task.

lar, how the child performed alone. For the poem, we coded whether the correct form was used and whether the lines rhymed as they were supposed to. For the map task we determined whether all pieces of information (street, direction, cross streets) were used to give directions and whether they were given in the correct order.

The results indicated that, for the map task, children whose mothers both had controlling attitudes and were in the high-pressure condition showed poorer performance than those in the other three groups. Thus, the results parallel those for mothers' behavior: When parents were oriented to the performance of their children, they were more controlling with them and the children did more poorly when they had to work on their own. Our interpretation of this finding is that when children interact with controlling mothers they are less likely to internalize what they learn and thus less able to apply it on their own. This, of course, defeats the purpose of having parents and children work together at home, which is to reinforce and solidify what is learned in school. There was no effect of condition on how accurate children were when writing their poem alone, but there was an effect for creativity. Children whose mothers came in with controlling attitudes and were assigned to the high-pressure condition wrote the least creative poems. There was indeed some evidence that the effect of condition was mediated by the mother's behavior: Children of mothers who were more controlling during the task had children who wrote accurate but uncreative poems when alone.

In general, the results of Grolnick et al.'s (2002) study show striking support for the idea that ego-involving parents in their children's performance leads to greater control, especially when the parents' attitudes are originally controlling. The fact that, on the map task, some mothers were more affected than others is reminiscent of Koestner, Bernieri, and Zuckerman's (1992) findings. They showed that more controlled individuals (those who are more oriented to signals about what they are supposed to do) are less consistent in their attitudes and behavior than are more autonomous individuals (those who are more oriented to their internal wants and desires). In Grolnick et al.'s (2002) study, mothers who held controlling attitudes were especially vulnerable to the performance manipulation, whereas highly autonomy supportive mothers were less vulnerable to the manipulation. Thus, when academic or sports endeavors emphasize competition or evaluation, some parents will be more vulnerable to the effects of such pressures than others. The results also suggest that the effects of the environment on parents may differ according to the type of task in which dyads are engaged.

A final set of Grolnick et al.'s (2002) findings concerned the mothers' experiences in the high- and low-pressure conditions. That there were no differences between women in the two conditions in the amount of pressure they experienced while working with the child, in their enjoyment of the task, or in their feelings of competence in working with their child, is striking. Why would this be so different than the pressure we feel when ego involved in our own performance? Recall that Ryan (1982) found that when students were ego involved in their own performance they reported more feelings of pressure and tension and less enjoyment than when they were task involved. How are these two situations different? I suggest that when people are ego involved in their performance, they can only try harder to attempt to maintain their self-esteem. When parents or teachers are ego-involved in children's performance, they can push the child toward positive outcomes, thereby relieving their own pressure of evaluation. Thus, one can transfer the evaluation one feels into one's behavior with that other. By controlling the children, the mothers in the performance condition may have inadvertently lessened their own pressure. It may not be nearly as aversive to be ego involved in another's performance as in one's own, because there is an outlet, albeit a counterproductive one.

ARE PARENTS ESPECIALLY VULNERABLE TO BEING EGO INVOLVED?

In this last section I present ideas based on evolutionary thinking. I ask this question: Are there built-in "hooks" that make many parents especially vulnerable to acting in ego-involved and controlling ways with their children?

There are many ways in which the parent–child relationship is special when compared with various other relationships. Parents usually live with their children, have the primary responsibility for teaching their children how to live in the world, and know more about their children than do others. Children share 50% of their genes with each biological parent, and that, too, makes for a special situation. Supporting the special nature of this relationship is research showing that parents think and feel differently about parenting their own versus others' children (Dawber & Kuczynski, 1999). Dawber and Kuczynski (1999) interviewed mothers of 5- to 9-year olds about how they would react to various situations with their own child, their child's best friend, or an unfamiliar child. Mothers felt more responsible for their own child's behavior and had more long-term goals for their own child versus for the unfamiliar child or their child's best friend. Mothers said they would be more upset if their own child transgressed relative to the friend or the unfamiliar child. "Ownness" is clearly a special category for parents.

I argue that indeed there are built-in "hooks." From the viewpoint of biology, parents are invested in their children's welfare, in their offspring surviving and reproducing. There is no doubt that evolution has selected for parents to be invested in their children. How else would it be possible for parents to make the sacrifices they make? Robert Trivers (1974) coined the term *parental investment*, which he defined as any investment in an individual offspring that increases the offspring's chance of surviving and reproductive success at the cost of the parent's ability to invest in other offspring. Inherent in this concept is the idea that parents have only a finite amount of resources to invest in offspring, themselves, and potential future offspring.

There is much evidence that humans, as a species, are adapted for high-investment parenting. C. Owen Lovejoy (1981) described different patterns of parenting in different species. One of these is associated with R-selected pattern species, which evolved in response to highly unstable environments where there was little predictability of resources. The greatest likelihood of offspring surviving and passing down their genes was for parents to have many offspring and to give each very little in terms of time, care, and resources. Some of the offspring will survive and others may not, but the best bet is on quantity, not quality, of offspring. Time and energy are expended on childbearing rather than childcaring. For example, some parents of insects simply deposit their eggs on the host plant and then depart, never to be seen again.

Another pattern is K selection. These species evolved in stable environments. They have low fertility rates—fewer offspring than biologically possible—yet they invest highly in them. They put forth time and energy to produce highly competitive offspring, which are more likely to survive and reproduce than others. Insects that are K selected may stand guard over their eggs to protect them from predators and then may carry their newly hatched young around in pouches on their abdomens. This pattern is seen in some species of birds, such as the great parent tit. She brings an average of one item of food to the nest every 30 sec of daylight. Each time she goes out she endures some risk to herself.

Lovejoy (1981) described humans as K-selected species. We do have fewer babies than is biologically possible, and we are adapted to invest high amounts of time and energy. In turn, our children are adapted to this high-investment parenting in that they have long periods of helplessness and an inability to survive on their own. This protracted period of helplessness in the context of high-investment parenting assures an extended period of learning.

Along with this pattern of parenting there must be selected for a mechanism in our brains to carry this out. In a highly adapted species such as humans, it is not genes that govern behavior on a moment-to-moment basis, but brains. These mechanisms within our brains are feelings. As author Robert Wright (1994) put it, "emotions are evolution's executioners."

Kevin MacDonald (1988), a proponent of bringing sociobiological perspectives to developmental psychology, suggests that the human affectional system
has evolved to keep family relationships close. In an evolutionary sense, it has
been selected for because it results in parents' investment in their children and
in the increased survival and reproduction of offspring. MacDonald described
this system as a reward system—not in the tangible reward sense, but rather in
the rewarding sense—in which being close with others, especially those related
to us, feels pleasurable and positive. Being with one's child feels good. Being separated from her feels awful. Anyone who has ever had to leave a premature baby
in an incubator knows the intense feelings of loss the separation evokes. On the
positive side, parents feel intense love and caring for their children, making being together a positive thing. Such feelings make parents *want* to sacrifice for
their children, to invest time and energy. Evolution has also resulted in a parallel
system in children in which they find cuddling, contact, and closeness with the
parent positive. This system of mutual affection and closeness allows for the invested parenting and learning that make for successful reproduction.

We have already seen that the warmth, time, and energy parents put into
their parenting pays off. Early on, I described the myriad studies showing that
warm, involved parenting is associated with a more cooperative child, a more
developed conscience, and lower levels of delinquency and aggressive behavior.

How does this relate to control? Are we adapted to be controlling with our
children? The answer to this question, I believe, lies in the flexible nature of the
parental investment system. Lovejoy (1981) suggested that although humans' selection is for high-investment parenting, the system is also a flexible one in which
the type of investment is dependent on cues in the environment. When cues suggest adverse conditions, and competition for survival, there is especially high investment. If cues suggest more optimal conditions, and low competition, there is
less investment. For example, Wilson (1975) described a particular beetle that
lives in an extreme environment for an insect, the intertidal mud of the northern
coast of Europe, where it constantly faces the hazards of high salinity and oxygen
shortage. The parents are exceptional in the amount of care given by the female
to the brood. She keeps the larvae in a burrow, protects them from intruders and
brings them fresh algae at frequent intervals. Such a flexible system would have
been highly adaptive in the environment in which humans evolved (a
hunter–gatherer society in which predators were likely) because a competitive,
adverse environment might mean death for offspring and no reproduction. Thus,
very high parental investment in stressful times was critical in the environment of
evolutionary adaptedness (EEA), because survival was on the line.

What about today? In real terms, we do not live in a particularly competitive
environment from the standpoint of our ancestors. Children do not have to

compete for survival in the way they must have in the environment in which we evolved. For the early humans, running faster than one's peers might have been the difference between being eaten by a lion and not. In our current environment there are surely consequences to running fast, but those do not necessarily include survival.

I suggest, however, that although the natural competitiveness is obviously decreased, manmade cues of competition abound. If one imagines the cues parents encounter in Western society, one can see how the system can go awry. Our schools and other institutions, such as organized sports, are set up as hierarchies with evaluation, social comparison, and "weeding out" as part of routine practice (Labaree, 1997). Indeed, Labaree (1997) argued that the goals of education have moved from obtaining knowledge that will be useful for children in their futures to obtaining credentials that will give them an edge over the competition. Rick Wolff (1997) described the world of sports as a pyramid, a narrowing process, such that many children may play at the elementary level, fewer in high school, and still fewer at the college level. Even in the very early years, parents get the message that they have to train their children early: Get that child into a quality preschool at age 4; make sure the child is swimming competitively by age 5. Otherwise, chances for success are slim.

Thus, in the EEA, determining how much to overprotect offspring and how much to do for them was adaptive. Survival was on the line. However, in the current context, in which competition is largely manmade, I argue that this flexibility in our genes, which causes us to act on cues of adversity and competition, is no longer adaptive. Barkow (1980) suggested that because our genes are the result of evolution that took place millions of years ago, characteristics that were adaptive in the EEA may no longer be adaptive in a new environment. To illustrate this point, Dawkins (1976) used the example of the sweet tooth. The sweet tooth was an adaptive mechanism when fruits and berries, necessary for survival, were the sweets to be found. Today, in the context of chocolate and processed sugar, the sweet tooth leads to obesity and high cholesterol. In the same way, the overcontrolling stance assumed by parents when they pick up cues of competition can now backfire. What was adaptive in the EEA may now lead to more control than is adaptive.

How are the cues of competition translated into control? When parents experience a competitive environment, they are likely to feel that their children are at risk or threatened. The combination of intense love and caring and wanting the best for our children, and the feeling of threat for our children, that they may not survive and thrive, easily translate into the feelings of concern, worry and competition that I described at the beginning of the chapter. That worry and concern result in the clenched fists at soccer games, surreptitious ways of finding out how other children are performing in school, and subtly asking other kindergartners' parents whether their children can read, as well as myriad other controlling behaviors. When parents acknowledge these controlling behaviors by saying "I only want the best for my child," "I can't let her throw away her talent," or "She's too young to know what she wants—she'll thank me later," they mean what they say. Their attempts to make sure their children do all they can are motivated by love and fear.

Part of the argument I advance here is that the threat parents experience translates into increased control. The link between threat and control, although only recently studied with regard to parenting in my laboratory and in Eva Pomerantz's at the University of Illinois, has been addressed for some time in the political psychology literature.

Stephen Sales, in a series of studies in the 1970s, reasoned that the more people experienced threat in their environments, the more authoritarian their orientations would be. Authoritarianism was characterized in the original way Adorno and his colleagues suggested (e.g., Adorno, Frenkel-Brunswik, Levinson, & Sanford, 1950) by terms such as *aggressive, domineering, closed,* and *tries to impose his will on others,* and indexed in a number of ways in these studies.

In 1972 Sales examined the effect of the Great Depression on conversion rates among church denominations. He compared the period from 1920 to 1929, a time of relative prosperity, to the period from 1930 to 1939, the Depression period. Sales found that conversion rates from nonauthoritarian to authoritarian churches increased during the period of presumed societal threat relative to the low-threat period. He then replicated this study for relatively good and bad economic years in Seattle, Washington, and obtained similar results. Doty, Peterson, and Winter (1991) more recently identified periods of relative high threat (1978–1982) and low threat (1983–1987) using income and the Consumer Price Index indicators, as well as high-impact news stories, such the Three Mile Island disaster, the Soviet invasion of Afghanistan, and the seizure of the American embassy in Tehran. The authors showed that societal measures of authoritarian syndrome, such as the purchase of attack dogs, cynicism, and acceptance of capital punishment, decreased between the high- and low-threat periods.

Sales and Friend (1973) looked also at individual-level effects. In two studies, participants were induced to succeed or fail on purported measures of intelligence and ability. Failure increased participants' level of authoritarianism; success decreased it.

In a more complex model, Feldman and Stenner (1997) suggested that threat would not have a direct impact on authoritarianism (authoritarianism is a personality variable and thus presumed to be static) but rather would activate authoritarian behavior in individuals with an authoritarian tendency. Individuals with an authoritarian tendency (conformist childrearing values) who perceived more economic and political threat were more ethnocentric and reported more punitive attitudes than individuals with a high authoritarian tendency but low perceived threat. There was no effect of threat on individuals with low authoritarian tendencies. In fact, if anything, low-authoritarian individuals showed more liberal responses under higher threat. The results suggest that threat polarizes, making some individuals more authoritarian, and others less.

Suzanne Gurland and I (Grolnick & Gurland, 1999) developed a questionnaire for parents that asked them about their views of the world their children will inhabit in the future. Among the subscales are (a) concern about the future (e.g., "Thinking about kids today, it's scary to imagine what the world will be like for them in the future," (b) harsh world (e.g., "It's getting harder and harder all the time to make a decent living," (c) perceived competition (e.g., "It's competitive out there; only some kids can make it"). We also measured parents' values for their children using M. L. Kohn's (1977) scale, which asks parents to rank order values such as obedience, which is more control oriented, and responsibility, which is more autonomy oriented. Parents reported on their autonomy supportive versus controlling behaviors using a scale developed for this study called the Parent Attitude Scale and the Children's Report of Parents' Behavior Inventory (Schaefer, 1965a). Parents also completed the General Causality Orientations Scale (Deci & Ryan, 1985a), which asks about people's tendency when making decisions to consider external factors, such as money, prestige, and what others think, versus internal factors, such as one's interest and opportunities for growth.

We predicted that parents who were more concerned about the future and those who saw the world as harsher and more competitive would display more controlling attitudes and behavior than those who saw the world as less harsh and competitive and who were less concerned (Grolnick & Gurland, 1999). Data from 40 participants supported some of the predicted relations (see Table 8.1). Parents who were more concerned about the future tended to be more likely to value obedience than those who were less concerned about the future. There were also marginally significant trends for parenting behavior, with parents more concerned about the future reporting more psychological control and less autonomy support. Finally, the results for the General Causality Orientations Scale (Deci & Ryan, 1985a) are intriguing: More control-oriented individuals perceived more competition and perceived the world their children will inhabit as more harsh than those lower in this orientation.

Pomerantz and Eaton (2001) assessed how much parents worried about their children's academic performance by asking them first to indicate the lowest grade that would be okay with them for their children to receive and,

TABLE 8.1

Correlations: Perceived Threat and Parents' Values and Behaviors

Category	Variable	Perceived Threat
Parent attitudes	Psychological control	.24
	Autonomy support	−.36**
Parent values	Obedience	.30**
	Autonomy	−.13
Parent behavior (laboratory)	Verbal autonomy support	−.40***
	Nonverbal autonomy support	−.24
GCOS	Autonomy	−.39***
	Control	.36**
	Impersonal	.23
Children's grades		−.29*

Note. GCOS = General Causality Orientations Scale.
$*p < .10, **p < .05, ***p < .01.$

second, how much they worry about whether their children will meet the standards they set. They also assessed parents' beliefs about control and the extent to which parents used controlling parenting practices. The results showed that the more parents worried about performance, the more they thought it was good to be controlling with children and the more they reported using controlling behaviors.

The results provide some support for the idea that one of the reasons parents become controlling is that they experience threat for their children (Grolnick & Gurland, 1999). Because they are invested in their children's performance, they tend to push them to achieve. In parents' minds, the push is perceived as something they almost have to do because they care about their children. This point is illustrated by my own experience in working with parents: Their justifications for the use of control center around their desire for the best for their children. They want their children to get all that they deserve. Because they are so embroiled in our cultural surroundings, these parents are unlikely to see the shaping effects the competitive institutions around them have on their goals for their children. The model of interaction between cues in our social contexts and parents' propensities to be invested in their children suggests that the context in which parents find themselves may be a key to how their investment translates into behavior.

HAVE THINGS CHANGED? POSSIBLE HISTORICAL INFLUENCES ON PARENTS' EGO INVOLVEMENT

If the evolutionary argument is true, then parents have always been invested in their children thriving. However, within this continuity there are historical changes in what parents expect to get back from their children. Consciously or unconsciously, parents want certain things from their children, whether love, support, or pride. How has history changed what parents expect from their children?

One major change is that, traditionally, parents could expect children to contribute financially to the family. In traditional families, children help support the family by working. Children in rural India and Brazil, for example, begin working for money by age 5 or 6 and are sizable contributors by the time they are 12. In this case, it makes sense for families to have many children, for they get a great deal back from their investment in the child. Data on childrearing have in fact supported this. For example, in traditional farm families children had a greater opportunity to contribute to the family income than children in urban families. Accordingly, in the past, as early as the 1400s and as late as the 1800s, farm families were always larger than urban families. With the advent of technology and the introduction of universal schooling in the late 19th century, the situation changed. Today, because children on farms cannot run large machines, and because they are in school for the majority of the day, they no longer contribute in major ways. Accordingly, farm families are no longer larger than urban families.

Furthermore, in the past parents could expect their children to take care of them in their older years. Through history, children have been a major help to elderly parents. Elderly people have frequently lived with their children, who care for them when they are ill and provide food and other support. In the United States, as recently as the 1940s, about 25% of people over age 65 lived alone (Michael, Fuchs, & Scott, 1980). With the advent of public transfer payments to the elderly, and parents' beliefs that they will be cared for by Social Security, retirement funds and other programs, and the geographic dispersion and mobility of the population, parents are more likely to believe they will live apart from their children. Retirement communities have flourished in the last 20 years.

What effect does this have on parents? I argue that the high financial and emotional investment parents make and the lack of financial return emphasize the psychological gain that parents expect back from children. Parents of today are more likely to anticipate feeling proud. They expect to get back love and loyalty from their children. This is made explicit in the Jewish religion. Jewish children are expected to provide their parents with *naches* (i.e., desired rewards) in the form of achievement, financial success, and grandchildren.

What does our historical diversion suggest? Possibly that, along with stressful times and competitive institutions, our current place in history makes parents especially at risk for investing psychologically in their children's performance. Thus, parents may need to be especially wary of how vulnerable they are to acting in controlling ways. Parents might see our current hierarchical institutions and competitive world as a setup that they must counter in highly conscious and active ways to maintain an autonomy supportive stance with their children.

9

Control and Academics

Jane Johnson had grown up in a poor neighborhood, but she had studied hard and done well in school and now had succeeded in the business world. Every evening she sat down with her son, Evan, doing paperwork as he did his homework. She corrected and cajoled him, calling herself his "homework buddy." Whenever he was assigned projects, she brainstormed, did Internet research, and was often up late cutting and pasting—long after he'd gone to bed. When she went away on a business trip, however, Evan fell behind in his work. His teacher complained to the parents about the spottiness of his homework. Jane and her husband quarreled. Jane was angry with him for not helping Evan more. Her husband, however, felt that Jane was controlling Evan's work and that as a result, their son hadn't developed his own approaches. "You're not going to be there in college, telling him what to do and when to do it!" her husband said.

There is no doubt that parental control plays out in large part in the area of academics. As we saw earlier, of all the domains important in a child's life, the one in which parents are most likely to use rewards is the area of academics (Boggiano et al., 1987). Many conflicts between parents and children center around homework or other school activities, and much parental strife is focused around children's school performance. In this chapter I focus first on why parental control might be detrimental to children's learning. Evidence presented earlier in the book showed that controlling styles are associated with lower levels of grades and achievement scores, and in this chapter I explain what it is about control that can undermine children's learning. Next I present an argument for why parents are so easily caught up in focusing on school performance. At the end of this chapter I offer some research-supported ideas to avoid traps that lead to control in academics.

HOW CONTROL UNDERMINES LEARNING

We have seen in the preceding chapters how parental control can weaken children's intrinsic motivation to pursue a variety of activities, among them school activities. There is also evidence that parental control can undermine children's movement toward a greater valuing of and personal sense of responsibility for behaviors and activities that are not inherently interesting, thus keeping children tied to external contingencies. But how does control relate to actual learning? I began asking this question when teachers in a school in which I was conducting a study began to challenge parts of this work.

After conducting a project on intrinsic motivation in an elementary school, I was giving feedback to teachers about the results of the study. Although I found the negative effects of parental control on children's motivation compelling, several of the teachers did not. "How about learning?" they asked. "That's the bottom line. Does control undermine children's learning?" At that time I could talk about the fact that controlling teacher styles were associated with lower grades and achievement test scores, but this did not really address the learning question. I thought at the time that it would be quite compelling to show that different learning contexts would result in different kinds of learning in children. Richard Ryan and I (Grolnick & Ryan, 1987) designed an experiment to look at just this.

Actually, there was a precedent for the work on which we were about to embark. Kenneth McGraw and John McCullers (1979) conducted a series of studies in the late 1970s demonstrating that instruction using extrinsic incentives facilitated a particular type of learning. In one study the authors had college students work with a type of problem activity originally used by Abraham Luchins (1942), in which students are given jars of different sizes and they have to end up with a specific amount of water in one jar by pouring water from the others. Students were given a set of nine problems with the same solution. The 10th problem, however, required the participants to "break set," because it could be solved only with a different, simpler solution. Half the participants were paid to work on these problems, and half were not. The participants who were paid had more difficulty "breaking set" or shifting to the new type of solution than the unpaid participants did. This was one of the first studies to show that rewards can impair the ability to think flexibly.

In my study with Richard Ryan (Grolnick & Ryan, 1987) we examined how children learned under varying amounts of control and pressure. Fifth-graders were given age-appropriate passages from a social studies book. They read under one of three conditions. In the *controlling-directed* condition they were told that they would be tested on the material and would receive a grade. Thus, children in this condition experienced pressure to perform. In the *noncontrolling directed* condition they were told that they would be asked questions later about the passage but that it would not be a test. Thus, although children realized that they needed to learn the material, they did not experience pressure. The focus was on learning the information. Finally, a third group (*nondirected*) was asked to read the passage to see what they thought about it. No mention was made about later questions.

After reading the passage under one of these conditions, children were assessed for their rote memory of the material ("Write down everything you can remember from the passage") as well as their conceptual understanding ("What was the main point of the passage?"). The results revealed that whereas children in the two directed conditions were equivalent in rote learning, children in the controlling-directed condition showed poorer conceptual understanding of the material.

Without forewarning, we returned to the classroom 2 weeks later and assessed the children's retention of the information they had learned in our study. At this time, we again asked the children to "write down everything you can remember from the passage you read." We found that children who read under the controlling-directed condition actually lost more information than children who read in either of the other two conditions (Grolnick & Ryan, 1987).

What do these studies tell us about the effects of pressure to perform? They both suggest that pressure, either in the form of rewards or evaluation, leads children to take a particular stance toward learning. When children learn under these conditions, the locus of their attention is on the outcome, the test, or getting the reward. Because of this, their attention is narrowed—their focus is on the details or the path to the easiest solution. This kind of orientation is at odds with conceptual understanding of material or problem solving, because both of these types of learning require flexibility, openness, and a broadening of perspective. McGraw and McCullers (1979) reviewed work on motivation and learning and suggested that control has different effects on two different types of tasks. *Algorithmic* tasks, which have a clear, rote solution, may not be undermined by controls, because narrowing of attention and a focus on details are not problematic. For example, if the task is a repetitive one, such as copying over words, rewards may not be undermining. However, *heuristic* tasks, which do not have straightforward solutions, and which require people to come up with their own unique solutions, are undermined by the narrowing of focus associated with controlling contexts. School activities such as creative writing, understanding the meaning of a story, or grasping and applying complex science concepts such as air pressure require more than "thinking within the box." They require activity, flexibility, and openness—characteristics of thinking that are clearly undermined by control and evaluation.

Furthermore, control appears to be at odds with retaining information. When children are pressured by a reward or by an evaluation, the material becomes a means to an end—a test is a good example. The information is not interesting on its own merit. Because the material was learned for the examination, once the test is over the information is no longer salient. Why should a logical mind retain it, or continue to process it? We have referred to this as the *core dump* phenomenon, in which information forced in is more likely to be dumped after completion of the program. In controlling contexts it is likely that children will not retain as much information as they would in autonomy supportive contexts.

The argument for the harmful effects of external constraints on conceptual learning and problem solving is also relevant to creative endeavors. Teresa Amabile has spent much of her career studying the factors that facilitate creativity. In her intrinsic motivation theory of creativity (Amabile, 1983), she suggested that people are most free to create when they are intrinsically motivated. In other words, people are at their most creative when they are engaged in a project because of interest and enjoyment and when they are feeling free to pursue their own goals and ideas. This is as likely to be true for children using crayons as it is for adults inventing a new recipe, or writers developing a new genre. Amabile (1983) went on to argue that factors that undermine intrinsic motivation, such as pressure, rewards, and evaluation, should also undermine creativity. In one study (Amabile, 1979), she asked college students to create collages with a number of available materials. Other students rated these collages on how creative they thought they were. Amabile found that students produced less creative collages when they expected to be evaluated than when they did not. In a related study, Koestner et al. (1984) showed that children's artwork was less creative under controlling conditions than it was in autonomy supportive environments. Amabile (1983) argued that creativity requires a playfulness and deep level of attention that are absent when rewards or evaluation are present. Such conditions distract individuals and narrow their focus toward the conventional. Both are at odds with creative expression.

We recently put these ideas to the test in a parent–child task (Grolnick, Gurland, DeCourcey, & Jacob, 2002). Would more controlling versus autonomy supportive parent–child interactions lead to different types of learning in children? In this study, discussed in part in Chapter 8, 60 mothers and their third-grade children were given the homeworklike tasks of learning to give directions on a map and writing a quatrain poem together. Mothers and children completed these assignments under one of two conditions: a high-pressure condition, in which mothers were led to believe their child would be tested and evaluated, or a low-pressure condition, in which evaluation and parental responsibility for the child's performance were de-emphasized. Mothers' levels of controlling and autonomy supportive behaviors were coded during the interaction. Of great interest here is the fact that, after the mother and child completed the task together, children were given a task to do on their own. Mothers left the room, and children either had to write their own quatrain or give someone directions to follow on a map, based on what they had learned while with their mothers. Map directions were coded for accuracy. The poems were rated for their adherence to the form as well as their creativity.

The important question here is: Does controlling behavior on the part of mothers undermine generalization of learning when children have to complete tasks on their own? After all, the goal of parents and children interacting when completing homework (or any learning task) is to provide an experience in which children's understanding and knowledge are increased, solidified, and taken back into the classroom. Another of our goals was to determine whether parental control interferes with children's creativity.

In regard to writing the poem, we found that neither the condition under which mothers worked nor the level of controlling behavior in the interaction predicted whether children used the correct form of the poem on their own. However, children whose mothers were more controlling in the interaction wrote less creative poems on their own. When parents push and pressure children, they may thwart their children's creativity.

For the map task, children of mothers who interacted under the high-pressure condition were less accurate in giving directions when they were asked to do so on their own. This was a compelling outcome. The information that children obtained under the controlling condition was not generalized so that it could be applied later. I argue that these results suggest that the type of learning that results under controlling conditions is less likely to be retained.

In short, the challenge that the elementary school teachers gave me to determine whether control affects learning set in motion of series of meaningful studies. Given the work I and others have done since that day, I can now confidently tell school administrators, teachers, and parents that control and evaluation undermine conceptual learning and the retention and generalization of information, which all are ultimately crucial to children's academic success. Understanding this, it is not surprising that controlling parenting is associated with lower grades and achievement scores. Although in the short run controls can facilitate rote memorization, the long-term effect of narrowed attention and lack of retention is to impair the development of an integrated knowledge base.

Earlier in this book I discussed the ways in which parental focus on children's performance and becoming ego involved—hinging their own feelings about themselves on how well their children perform—leads to greater control. When parents become hooked into focusing on their children's performance, they are at risk for using the kinds of pressures and bribes that undermine motivation and conceptual learning. As I argue in the next section, the area of academics unfortunately is especially ripe for controlling parental involvement. The reasons for this are numerous.

WHY PARENTS BECOME HOOKED INTO ACADEMICS

A friend recently told me about a parent–teacher conference at her daughter's school. During the meeting, the teacher talked about a number of positive accomplishments. "She's improving in social studies," the teacher said, "but she's having some difficulties grasping the math concepts I've been presenting this month." Suddenly my friend felt the sting of tears in her eyes. "It was just a normal parent–teacher conference," she said. "How could I become so teary eyed?" She was surprised at how emotionally invested she was in her daughter doing well.

Why do parents become so ego involved in their children's school performance? Here I will focus on two important reasons. The first is our culturally based emphasis on intelligence. It is important to understand how our fascination with and view of intelligence may push parents to get hooked into children's school performance. A second explanation is that American schools are highly competitive and hierarchical, constantly sorting out who is better than whom. Such a competitive situation makes it easy for parents to become focused on their children's performance. It is easy for parents to get caught up in such a highly charged, competitive atmosphere.

Intelligence As a Trait

Sarah Harkness and Charles Super (1997) conducted a fascinating study about how parents from different cultures see their children. When they interviewed American parents and asked them straightforwardly to describe their children, the American parents used terms such as *bright, intelligent,* and *smart.* It was obvious from these interviews that the dimension of intelligence is highly prized by American parents. This is a key manner in which parents define their children. In contrast, parents interviewed in Holland described their children through a completely different trait: regularity—in other words, whether or not the child ate and slept at the same time each day. For these parents, the trait of regularity is both highly salient and highly valued.

So if American parents are intent on developing intelligent children, how does this translate into ego involvement? Part of the answer to this question concerns the way in which we view intelligence. Carol Dweck and her colleagues (e.g., Bandura & Dweck, 1985; Dweck & Leggett, 1988) have suggested that some individuals see intelligence as something that people have, a fixed trait that can't be changed. Children who have this "entity" view of intelligence are quite focused in their school goals on proving that they have ability. If intelligence is something that one can't change, then it makes sense that one would be invested in having it and showing others that one has it, and children, in the way they approach tasks, do just this. For example, if given an opportunity to pursue easy work that they will get right or more challenging work from which they are likely to learn, children with entity views of intelligence pick the easy work that will show that they are smart. On the other hand, some individuals view intelligence as malleable, something one can increase. Children with such a view are most likely to set learning goals for themselves and want to engage in tasks that increase their skills. They are more likely to pick challenging work that will teach them something relative to easy work that will show they are smart.

Like the children just described, any parent in U.S. culture (and this includes most parents) who is focused on the importance of intelligence, especially parents who hold the "entity" view, are vulnerable to latching onto their children's performance and thus becoming controlling. Just as children who hold the entity view wish to prove their abilities, parents who hold such views may be focused on making sure their children come across as smart. The result of such a concentration may be parents who become worried and concerned about documenting that their children "have it." These parents become highly threatened by failure and negative feedback. This may make it more likely that parents give children answers on their homework and push them to take the easiest route that will give them the best outcome. When parents engage in such behaviors, children come to themselves become concerned with demonstrating their abilities and have difficulties when faced with challenge or failure (Pomerantz & Eaton, 2001). When parents have a notion of fixed intelligence they are also more likely to give children the message that doing well is a more important goal than working hard and learning. In theory, parents know that learning is key. However, having an entity theory and being part of a culture that stresses intelligence may propel parents to replace the goal of helping children learn with the goal of making sure that the children's grades look good. When intelligence is viewed as something that can be increased, parents may be less likely to be threatened by poor performance and less likely to fall into the trap of getting hooked on outcomes.

Cultures differ in regard to how intelligence is typically perceived. Asian cultures, for example, see effort as being a major part of intelligence—much more so than Americans do (H. W. Stevenson et al., 1990). Although there are no data to support this, it may be that Asian parents are more interested in learning than performance and may be less vulnerable to ego involvement.

Competitive Schools

In U.S. culture evaluation is central to the enterprise of schooling. Schools are charged with the task of determining who is doing well and who is not. Children begin their academic careers with kindergarten screenings designed to evaluate their readiness for school. From there, the evaluation continues and, although the evaluation may be more formal in some schools than in others, it nonetheless is pervasive. In traditional schools, evaluation is evidenced by grades, stickers, gold stars, ability groupings, and work displayed on bulletin boards. In addition to grades, evaluation is conducted in more subtle forms, such as on whom the teacher calls, whom she decides to help, and how long she waits for a child's response. Comments on children's papers such as "good try" and "keep working" send messages clearly understood by parents.

Deborah Stipek and Douglas Mac Iver (1989) suggested that the nature of evaluation changes over children's years of schooling. In the preschool years, children tend to move around a great deal, engaging in different activities at different times, which makes comparisons less salient. Furthermore, evaluation is almost always positive. The feedback that parents receive from preschool teachers is rarely negative and is based more on behavior than on the substance of children's work. As children enter the elementary school years they tend to be given the same assignments. Evaluation comes to be based more on getting the right answer, rather than making an effort. Tangible feedback is both positive and negative. By the age of 7–8 years, children actively compare their performance with that of others. They use the feedback to evaluate their own competencies. They are now part of the culture of evaluation of schools.

Along with their children, parents clearly feel the evaluation pressure of schools, as teachers are well aware. One teacher I interviewed told me that she used to have parent volunteers in her classroom. However, one day as she was entering the room after a brief errand, she caught a parent peeking in her grade book. She noticed that some parents who volunteered craned their necks to look at other children's papers "to see what [grades] they got." Because of this, she now uses only volunteers who have children in different classrooms. Clearly, parents become hooked into the competition inherent in the school environment.

Sociologist David Labaree (1997) has been highly critical of what he calls the *credentialing model* of schools. His critique rests on the argument that schools stress educational distinctions and grades more than learning. In the credentialing model the goal of education is not so much to attain useful knowledge as it is to gain a competitive advantage over others by acquiring a "badge of merit" that will distinguish one person from others. In such a situation, the formal characteristics of schooling—grades, credits, degrees—receive greater weight than the substance. Furthermore, the structure of schools takes on a more hierarchical shape in which schools provide ways in which students can raise themselves up. Teaching takes a back seat to sorting.

I would argue that a school environment that stresses comparison and grades—the outcome of which holds the key to opportunities for success in U.S. society—is one that invites parents to focus on children's performance. In turn, the parents feel compelled to push and pressure their children. As Labaree (1997) argued, these badges of merit have real consequences for the doors that will open for children in their futures. Because parents love their children and want only the best for them, it is easy to see how they fall into the trap of focusing on products and not process in dealing with their children's school lives. If my earlier argument that parents are predisposed to monitor the competitiveness of the environment in which their children live, and respond accordingly holds, then it is no wonder that the school context is the arena in which control is most likely.

INVOLVEMENT VERSUS CONTROL: A REPRIEVE

Thus far I have stressed the undermining effects of control on children's motivation and school learning. At this point the reader may be asking whether the answer is for parents to keep their hands off—hands off homework, hands off report cards, and minimal contact with schools. To this idea, I reply with a resounding "NO." The literature backs me up on this. Although many bodies of literature are ambiguous with respect to results, such is not the case for research on parent involvement. Across the full age range of children, studies indicate that when parents are involved, children do better in school. For example, at the preschool level, Reynolds, Mavrogenes, Bezruczko, and Hageman (1996) showed that parent involvement in a preschool program predicted academic outcomes for low-income minority children. Barbara Tizard and her colleagues (Tizard, Blatchford, Burke, Farquhar, & Plewis, 1988) showed that children from homes with high numbers of books and a high frequency of reading activities outperform their age-mates in writing.

For school-age children the results are equally compelling. In a national sample of children ranging in age from 5 to 17, D. Stevenson and Baker (1987) showed that children whose parents were more involved were more successful in school than children whose parents were less involved. Furthermore, some of the effects of family background appear to be explainable by levels of parent involvement in these families. In other words, some of the reason that children of parents with low levels of education themselves are not doing as well as those of parents with more education is that the parents with low levels of education are less involved. Joyce Epstein (1983) showed that students whose teachers and parents used frequent parent-involvement practices (e.g., volunteering in the classroom, sending home work for parents and children to complete together) reported more positive attitudes toward school, better homework habits, and more homework completed on weekends.

In a study of 11- to 14-year-old children, my colleague and I (Grolnick & Slowiaczek, 1994) measured three types of parental involvement. The first was involvement at school, which included going to school activities and events and volunteering in the classroom. The second was involvement in intellectual activities at home, which meant engaging in activities such as talking about current events with children and going to the library. The third type was personal involvement, which included knowing about the child's school experiences, such as when report cards come out, the names of the other children in the class, and so forth. We then measured children's attitudes and motivations regarding school and their levels of achievement and grades. We found that, when parents are more involved intellectually and at school, children feel more competent in school and feel more in control of their school successes and failures. These motivational characteristics translate into greater school achievement.

The reader might argue that parental involvement is a developmental phenomenon—that parents should begin with high levels of involvement, which might have positive effects, and then decrease that involvement so that children are on their own in the later years. Perhaps in the later years involvement has a negative impact, similar to that of control. One study on the transition to junior high school suggests that this may not be so (Grolnick, Kurowski, Dunlap, & Hevey, 2000). Grolnick et al. (2000) looked at the transition to junior high because this change can be stressful for children. Many experience disruptions in their self-esteem and academic performance. The reasons for these disruptions may involve the nature of this transition. In many cases students transition from small, intimate elementary schools to larger, more bureaucratic junior high schools where they know fewer children and where, because they have multiple teachers, they do not get to know their teachers in a personal way. Carol Midgely and her colleagues (e.g., Midgely & Feldlaufer, 1987) have further shown that, although students prefer more opportunities for autonomous functioning as they get older, there is more regimentation, more control, and fewer opportunities for input in the junior high context. All of these factors, along with the simultaneous bodily changes occurring in early adolescence, make this a vulnerable time for children.

Grolnick et al. (2000) wondered whether parent involvement could buffer children from experiencing some of the negative sequelae of the transition to junior high. To answer this question, we assessed parents' levels of involvement and children's motivation and performance when the children were in sixth grade and after they had transitioned to junior high in seventh grade. In fact, we did find that for many students there were declines in grades and feelings of competence over the transition. However, as we predicted, children whose mothers were more involved with their children in intellectual activities at home in sixth grade did not show the same declines in feelings of competence in school and in reading grades as did children whose parents were less involved. Children whose mothers were higher in personal involvement were less likely to drop in reading grades and less likely to show increased acting-out and learning problems in the classroom. Furthermore, it was not just involvement at sixth grade that proved important but whether mothers remained involved as their children made the transition to junior high. Mothers who increased or maintained their involvement had children who did not decrease in feelings of self-worth over the transition. Involvement clearly plays a key role in children's school success through the junior high years.

The research I have presented underscores the fact that involvement affects children by giving them direct help, which in turn improves their school performance. Involvement also affects their attitudes and motivations for school. When parents are involved, they convey their value for school, their confidence in the child's abilities, and their attitude that school challenges can be met head on. These messages clearly affect children's approach to and engagement in school.

There is another way in which parent involvement helps children. From parents and others in their environments children learn how the "school game" works—for example, how grades are connected to later choices. They learn how to negotiate the choices that are offered in middle school and high school to maximize their learning and future success. It is easy to imagine how more advantaged families are more likely to have and pass on this information to their children than are less educationally advantaged families. For example, more advantaged parents, who themselves have had the opportunity to go to college, have knowledge about the consequences of a poor grade in school for college applications. They have an idea of how choices in school, such as whether to take pre-algebra or calculus, affect future opportunities after high school. When parents communicate this information to children, the children have a better chance of succeeding in the educational enterprise. Parents are the conveyors of subtle information that makes a difference.

Parent involvement in children's schooling is clearly a goal for all families. Of course, consistent with earlier chapters, I argue that involvement that is supportive of children's autonomy not only is possible, but it is also likely to be associated with the best performance, motivation, and long-term success of children.

HOMEWORK: AN ILLUSTRATION

A friend of mine, a sensitive and supportive woman, told me about a shadow box project she recently did with her son. She described how she began in a patient manner, allowing her son to lead, providing help and assistance. However, the tension built as his cuts were not straight and his coloring not quite within the lines. By the end, when the shadow box didn't look as neat as she felt it should, she ripped the markers out of his hand and completed the project herself.

Many of us have been involved in homework battles with our children. In a study conducted in parents' homes (Grolnick et al., 1997), we interviewed 200 parents about their involvement in their children's schooling. These interviews happened to take place right after the school science fair. Some of the science projects were extremely elaborate. In fact, some that I saw looked downright professional. My first thought was what an enormous effort these parents had put into these projects. I was soon to learn more than I anticipated.

Parents could not talk about their experience enough. The stress they had experienced was evident in their voices. They described battles over different understandings of directions, over the focus of the project, over who would do what. These testimonies demonstrated how interaction can turn into a battle.

Although many such incidents between parents and children blow over quickly, fights over homework can get serious. They can become battlegrounds for parents with different philosophies about childrearing. The hypothetical family of Jim and Sarah and their daughter Rachel provide a perfect example of this situation. Sarah feels Rachel should take responsibility for her own work and should take the consequences at school if she does not finish it or if she does a sloppy job. Jim believes it is harmful to Rachel's self-esteem to allow her homework to be turned in incorrectly. He believes that he and Sarah should do anything they have to to ensure that the work is done and that it is correct. That includes doing it for her. The battle between the parents goes on daily, with Rachel in the middle. The situation has seriously strained Jim and Sarah's marriage.

Research on homework bears out the stress associated with homework time. Xu and Corno (1998) videotaped six families, two times each, engaged in homework with their third-graders. The sessions all evoked strong feelings—all children became upset or frustrated at least some of the time. Twelve of the 13 homework sessions involved strong, emotionally charged incidents involving four of the six families. At least 4 parents clearly became upset.

Why was this effect observed? Homework is clearly challenging for children, especially during the early grades, when homework is new for them. It is challenging for children to get started. They have to shift from nonschool to school- related activities, and then they must maintain their attention despite distractions and their desire to be doing other things. They also have to manage the emotions that emerge when they have difficulty understanding directions or solving problems. In short, homework involves the need for strategies to self-regulate. Parents play a key role in this process. Leone and Richards (1989), for example, found that students reported being more attentive to homework when completing it with a parent than when they are on their own or with a peer. Parents provide guidance in creating a homework environment that is free of distractions, in suggesting strategies for problem solving, and in helping children cope with difficulty and distractions, and the strategies parents suggest and model clearly have an impact. Xu and Corno (1998) found that the strategies children tend to use are ones their parents model, indicating that children do in fact internalize the strategies presented by their parents. For example, children in Xu and Corno's study were asked about the best time to do homework. Their answers corresponded almost exactly to the ideas expressed by their parents.

This situation, however, can be an opportunity to develop self-regulatory skills only when parents allow children to take responsibility for homework. They also need to help children develop strategies to be used on their own. For example, Xu and Corno (1998) found it useful when parents gave children choice in the order of assignments. Children also worked better when they had input into how their homework would be structured, for example, when to begin, how long of a break after school the child would have to gear up for starting homework, and in when and how long to take breaks. Homework time can be a time for positive parent–child interaction, modeling, and the development of self-regulation. Thus, it is important for parents to be highly involved in a way that supports children's autonomy during the homework process. Given this, an examination of how to be highly involved in homework and school more generally is timely. I now outline some strategies that parents can use.

1. Dealing With Stress

In chapter 7 parental control was traced back to levels of parental stress. Stress can lead to controlling interactions by usurping the time and energy necessary for autonomy support. When parents are engaged in multiple tasks, are time pressured, or simply under the constraints of work or home burdens, they cannot feel free to allow their children to problem solve, make mistakes, and go at their own pace. Parents in such conditions are unlikely to take children's perspective and follow their leads. Thus, in working with their children on schoolwork, parents will be most likely to provide an autonomy supportive context when they can minimize their own stress. When working with a child, it is useful to carve out a time and space that is not time pressured. In today's busy world this time may need to be planned ahead so that intrusions—psychological or physical—can be minimized.

2. Identifying Signs of Ego Involvement

When parents' feelings about themselves are tied to children's performance, controlling interactions involving pressure and solving problems for children are more likely. Thus, it is crucial for parents to identify the signs of this orientation. Indications of ego involvement include feelings of pressure and tension in the parent, irritability with the child's performance, and a desire to take over. Parents who recognize such signs can try to identify the issue with which they are struggling. For example: What is on the line for me if my child does not perform well? Will I feel like a bad mother or father? Do I feel the teacher will think I am a bad parent if the paper is turned in with errors?

3. Keeping the Focus on Learning

As discussed earlier, parents, in working with their children, can be oriented to their children's performance. They can be trying to make sure the outcome is right or that the child looks good, or they can be emphasizing the joy of learning. To avoid controlling interactions, parents can make as their goals a positive process in their interactions rather than a perfect product. A child, through working with the parent, is exposed to many messages. Some of these include what the parent thinks of the child's abilities, whether learning is aversive or fun, and whether it is okay to make mistakes or that errors should be avoided at all costs. When parents are oriented to their children's learning, they convey messages most conducive to learning orientations in their children. For example, consider the messages provided in two comments about a child's mistake. One parent says "No problem; try again." Another parent says "Next time, do it right the first time." A child comes home from school talking about what he learned in social studies. One parent immediately asks how the child did on his test. The other focuses on what the child thinks he learned. The messages conveyed by the second parent in each example shows a focus on the learning and on the importance of the child's effort—such an orientation, when picked up by the child, will make it more likely that children will persevere in difficult situations in the future.

4. Allowing Children to Take Responsibility

An example from my own "files" illustrates how difficult it is for parents to give over responsibility for their children's school performance. My elder daughter is good about doing her homework and typically asks for help when she has a problem with it. When she completes her homework, she puts it into her backpack, ready for the next day. I usually ask her whether she has completed her homework and whether she wants me to check it over. When she does not want it checked over, I find myself torn between checking it over anyway (when she is not looking) and allowing her to hand it in, warts and all. I have, I admit, sneaked a look at the work after she had gone to bed.

How difficult it can be at times for parents to recognize in an affective way that the homework is the child's, not theirs, that the report card reflects the child's work, not their own. In order for children to be responsible for doing their own work, parents need to allow them to choose whether and how to do their work and to accept the consequences of their actions. This is autonomy support. However, as I stressed in the early chapters of this book, taking an autonomy supportive stance does not mean being hands off. To succeed, children require the structure and information to be competent, conveyed in an autonomy supportive manner. Thus, parents might set up times for doing homework, set expectations for when and how homework is done, and describe the consequences of meeting or not meeting those expectations.

Such structure can be developed in an autonomy supportive manner, that is, including the child's input, empathizing with the child's perspective, and using noncontrolling language (i.e., avoiding *shoulds* and *have tos*). For example, a parent's expectation might be that homework is completed before any TV is watched. However, the child might convey his or her need to unwind for half an hour before beginning homework. The parent might empathize about how hard it is for the child to jump into homework right after school. Together, parent and child can work toward a structure that makes sense to both, for example, starting 1 hour after the child returns home from school. They can also work out together a set of consequences that will follow if homework is not done. Perhaps, for example, the consequence will be that the child will watch no TV at all the next night. This is quite different than the parent standing over the child to ensure that the homework is done. In the first instance, the child has the choice to meet the expectation, or to not meet it and suffer the consequence. In the second, the parent takes responsibility for the child's work. If parents' goals are to have children initiate and maintain their own behavior, then avoiding taking responsibility for children's actions is crucial. Of course, this might mean that parents need to live with some mistakes. To avoid taking responsibility for children's behavior, parents might set up an agreement and structure beforehand that allows children maximum responsibility.

5. Work Toward School Reform

As parents are well aware, there is much dissatisfaction with the state of American schools today. The rhetoric often comes in the form of accusations of low standards and lazy children. For many, the answer to school problems is a back-to-basics view: stricter controls, more pushing, tougher prodding. In short, this approach advocates more of what American schools have been doing up to now. However, as Alfie Kohn argued in his powerful book *The Schools Our Children Deserve* (1999), and as the research presented in this chapter attests, controls impair children's learning and their ability to retain information. More controls may increase children's performance on standardized tests, some of which tap memorization and short-term recall. However, these controls are unlikely to lead to the kind of learning that will make children knowledgeable adults who value and love learning. Parents must get into this debate. They must echo the voices of many top educators who stress that we can have high standards without controlling practices and that the old "receptacle model," according to which children are baskets that need to be filled up with knowledge, does not work. Parents must call for better schools. They cannot be satisfied with more of the same. They must not be afraid of new ideas.

10

Control and Sports

There is a not-uncommon scenario in my husband's orthopedics practice. Parents come in with a preteen or teenage female soccer player who complains about a persistently sore knee. After careful examination, my husband recommends that the girl refrain from playing for a specified amount of time. My husband watches the faces of the patient and her parents carefully. More than once, he has seen relief flood the girl's face. Worry lines wrinkle the parents' foreheads. "You don't mean she can't play at all," a parent might say. "Yes," he says. Inevitably, he later receives a telephone call asking if she might just play for a short time in this one terribly important game. It is always the parent looking for the loophole—never the girl.

In talking with people about the positive effects of autonomy support and the negative effects of control, both professionals and laypeople counter my research findings with examples of successful athletes. Anecdotes abound of parents who sacrifice their children's childhoods to go for the gold medal, who push their children hard to achieve goals that may not be the children's at all, and who scream loudly and criticize harshly. Many people believe that in order for a young athlete to achieve, the parents must be highly controlling. I felt so fortunate when, just as I was beginning this chapter, I stumbled onto Summer Sanders's book *Champions Are Raised, Not Born: How My Parents Made Me a Success* (1999). In this spirited volume Sanders, an Olympic gold medal swimmer, describes her parents and how they raised her. Indeed, as the subtitle indicates, she attributes her success to them.

In striking contrast to the myriad stories of successful athletes whose parents lived apart from them, who pushed them relentlessly, and who lived through them—and many of these biographies have sad endings—Sanders tells a very

134

different tale. Her parents supported her beyond what could be expected. They routinely got up at 5 a.m. to swim with her. They traveled across the country to attend her swim meets and competitions. But they never pushed her; neither did they set their sights on the gold.

> My parents never saw my talent or my competitive drives as an invitation to impose any ambitions on me. They were never in it for the medals on the wall.... They did not put a pool in our backyard to make me into a champion; whatever I wanted to do, they were behind me, matching their level of commitment to mine. (Sanders, 1999, p. 2)

When a mother shows off her daughter, bragging that she is a potential Olympian, Sanders wants the woman to

> understand that the only thing that'll take her daughter to the furthest edge of her potential is the sheer pleasure she takes in exercising her God-given ability. I want to talk to her about the true nature of motivation—how it is sparked by doing something fun, how it builds from doing something well, but how it can be snuffed out by parents who are too pushy, who are focused on the product rather than the process. (Sanders, 1999, p. 6)

Sanders's (1999) informal interviews with several Olympic athletes, including Bonnie Blair, Dan Jansen, Dot Richardson, and Matt Biondi, provide anecdotal evidence that the lore out there may be just that. There is another side to the story, perhaps a happier side.

CHILDREN AND SPORTS: A GROWING PREOCCUPATION

More than 20 million American youngsters ages 6–16 participate in organized sports programs each year. From Little League, to town soccer, to competitive swimming and skiing, the magnitude of children's participation in organized athletics has never been greater.

Before asking about how parenting may influence children's motivation in this area, it is important to know why children participate in sports in the first place. Wankel and Kreisel (1982) asked youths in amateur sports why they engaged in their sport activities. The major reasons were improvement of skills, a sense of personal accomplishment, and the excitement derived from the activity. Alderman and Wood (1976) found the primary motivators for young hockey players to be desires for competence, challenge, and affiliation. Another study identified learning and improving skills, having fun, being physically fit, making friends, and achievement as important motives for children to participate in sports (Gill, Gross, & Huddleston, 1983). One study, representing a variety of youth sports, such as soccer, football, baseball, basketball, and softball, found that having fun was the top reason children endorsed (H. Barber, Sukhi, & White, 1999).

I believe this is good news. The reasons children generally give for participating in sports are intrinsic ones. They don't do it for the trophies they will win or the praise they will get from those around them. They are excited about participating, and they wish to enhance their skills. Although this is the case for many children when they begin their sport, these same feelings and motives unfortunately may not continue. Children's lack of continued enthusiasm is illustrated in the high levels of withdrawal from sports as they get older. In North America it is not uncommon to lose 80%–90% of registered organized sports participants by 15 years of age (Orlick, 1978). Dropping out of sports is particularly common for adolescents (Roberts & Kleiber, 1982), especially girls (Brown, 1985). No doubt, this decrease in participation is a multidetermined phenomenon. What could be the reasons?

One of the reasons so many children withdraw from sports stems from the way in which sports are organized over the years of a child's life. Wolff (1997) described competitive sports as

> a natural pyramid of success ... On the bottom of that pyramid are all the wonderfully talented kids who play youth sports. But as you begin to climb that pyramid you find that only a certain percentage of those athletically gifted kids ever go on to become high school players. Then, going farther up the pyramid, the competition becomes even stiffer; only a small percentage of high school athletes are ever good enough to make a college team.... It's quite a narrowing process. (p. 12)

Whether the structure of competitive youth sports as a pyramid is "natural" in any way is certainly a point for debate. When you think about it, isn't the goal of sports widespread participation and enjoyment? However, there is no doubt that with the way sports are structured only some children can rise to the upper levels.

Coincident with this narrowing is a change in the nature of sporting. As children get older, sports settings become characterized by an increased emphasis on competence outcomes and normative ability—children are compared with others (S. A. White & Duda, 1994). The emphasis on winning increases, and there are more tangible consequences of those wins. Sports psychologist Terry Orlick (1978) described competitive sports as a "failure factory" that not only eliminates the "bad ones" but also turns off many of the "good ones." What are the ramifications of this emphasis on rewards, competition, and comparison?

REWARDS AND FEEDBACK

Just as rewards can undermine children's intrinsic motivation for school activities, they can be detrimental to recreational activities. Orlick and Mosher (1978) had 9- to 11-year-olds work with a stabilometer, a task that involves motor balancing. In general, children very much enjoy this task. Half of the children in this study received a reward for engaging in the task, and half did not. Four days later, the children returned to the laboratory and were given a chance to play on the stabilometer or to engage in other tasks. The children who had been rewarded previously spent less time engaging in the task than those who had not been rewarded. Just as with the other activities I have discussed, when children receive rewards they experience themselves as engaging in the activity for the reward rather than for its inherent enjoyment. Intrinsic motivation subsequently diminishes. Children's love for the activity fades away. It is replaced by a feeling of work in order to attain a reward.

Studies also show the importance of feedback children receive. For example, children playing on the stabilometer were given either positive or negative feedback as to how they were performing after every fourth trial (Vallerand & Reid, 1984). Those who got the positive feedback increased in their later motivation to pursue the task, whereas those who received negative feedback decreased in their intrinsic motivation. One study showed that losing does not necessarily undermine motivation—as long as one does not feel incompetent. McAuley and Tammen (1989) asked physical education students who had been matched for basketball shooting ability to play a game in which players attempt to make shots that their opponents would miss. At the end of the game, a winner and a loser were declared. After the game, students reported on how competent they felt at the game. They also reported on their intrinsic motivation to engage in the game. The results showed that the participants who felt successful (even if they lost) reported higher levels of intrinsic motivation than participants who felt unsuccessful. This study nicely illustrates how children can feel competent even if, objectively, the game was lost. It also shows how feelings of incompetence undermine motivation.

These results suggest that rewards and negative feedback that result in feelings of incompetence undermine children's motivation to pursue recreational activities that they initially described as fun and enjoyable. The structure of competitive sports, with its "weeding out," its trophies, and its advances, is clearly a setup for undermining motivation. What about the competition inherent in the games, which increases over the years?

COMPETITION

Parents are often concerned that, as their children move along in the world of sports, and competition becomes more intense, the children will begin to feel too pressured. They don't want their children's love of the sport to diminish. Playing soccer in the schoolyard may be great fun, but when the game becomes more serious, will it still be fun? How can parents increase the probability of keeping it an entertaining and positive endeavor?

One question is whether or not engaging in competitive sports in and of itself undermines motivation. Many people believe that, by definition, competition involves pressure—perhaps that in itself matters most. Perhaps how parents handle competition with their children can't make a difference.

In fact, early studies found that competition decreases intrinsic motivation. Deci, Betley, Kahle, Abrams, and Porac (1981) had pairs of college students work on puzzles with one of two sets of instructions (actually one in each pair was an experimental confederate posing as a participant). Participants were instructed either to "try to beat the other person"—the competitive set—or to try and "do their best"—obviously the noncompetitive set. In both groups the confederate had been instructed to let the participant win. So, both groups (those given the competitive set and those given the noncompetitive set) received positive feedback. Participants given the competitive set engaged in less puzzle solving during a free-choice period than did those who worked on the puzzles under the noncompetitive set. Thus, the results of Deci et al.'s (1981) study suggest that competition undermines intrinsic motivation.

More recent studies, however, have questioned this finding and have suggested that the effects of competition depend on a number of factors. Reeve and Deci (1996) reasoned that the effect of competition would depend on two factors: whether or not one wins (winning should increase feelings of competence and, thus, intrinsic motivation) and whether the competition is experienced as either controlling or informational. Controlling competition would be that which emphasizes the importance of winning or beating the opponent. Informational competition does not pressure one to win. To test out their ideas, Reeve and Deci asked 100 undergraduate students to work on Happy Cube puzzles with a confederate. Participants worked on the cubes in either a noncompetitive condition—"just do your individual best"—or in either pressure or no-pressure competitive conditions. In each of the competitive conditions the participants were told to "outperform the other by solving your puzzles faster than the other person." In one competitive condition, in which there was pressure to win, the experimenter added that

> it doesn't matter how fast or slow you solve each puzzle, and it doesn't matter whether you figure out how the puzzle works. The only thing that matters is which of you wins the competition. So focus all of your attention on being the winner.

After the competition there was a free-choice period during which participants had an opportunity to play with the Happy Cubes or to do another activity. The results suggested that there was no difference between participants who competed and those who did not. But there was a difference between those who competed in the pressure-to-win condition and those who competed in the no-pressure situation. Competitors who had not been pressured to win played with the new puzzle forms more than did competitors who had been pressured to win. Performance on the Happy Cubes did not differ for the experimental groups. The results also provided support for a process model, in which pressure to win decreases feelings of choice or self-determination for the activity, which then decreases intrinsic motivation.

What does this say about the world of children's sports? The good news is that the fact that there is competition within sports may not necessarily be negative. By definition, sports include competition—indeed, many of them could not be played without that factor. For example, if the tennis ball were directed right to the opponent each time, the challenge would be gone. However, the research has shown that when the goal becomes to win rather than to play well this emphasis harms children's intrinsic motivation. It is no wonder with the pressure and emphasis on winning that children drop out in such large numbers. In the next section I describe children's own approaches to sports and how they can erode the noble goals with which children begin their sporting careers.

CONSEQUENCES OF EGO INVOLVEMENT IN SPORTS

Parents and coaches are keenly aware that, by the time children are in elementary school, they differ greatly in the way they approach sports. Joan Duda (1992) suggested that one fundamental way in which children differ in the way they approach sports is how they define sport success and how they judge their own overall competence. For some children, success is determined by beating other children and being the best. Their focus is on where they stand in relation to other children. For others, their sense of success is based on their feelings of mastery and the extent to which they improve. The first set of children can be considered ego involved in their sport activities. They are concerned with their sports performance. Their egos are on the line in each game. Losing out has ramifications for how they feel about themselves. The second set of children can be said to be task involved, because they are focused on the game itself. When they are not successful, they may be unhappy, but they don't necessarily feel bad about themselves.

S. A. White, Duda, and Keller (1998) identified children who were either ego involved or task involved and asked these children what was important to them about participating in sports. In particular, they were asked to endorse different responses to the question "A very important thing sport should do ..." Naturally there was a range of responses. Some youngsters chose to emphasize self-esteem and sport ethos (e.g., sport gives us self-confidence, gives us a chance to feel like a champion). Others endorsed social status and popularity (e.g., sport helps us to move into a job that will pay us good money; sport helps us to be popular among our friends). Another response talked about good citizenship (e.g., sport teaches us to respect adults). Still others focused on deception and superiority (e.g., sport teaches us how to bend the rules when necessary and weed out those who don't have what it takes). The results showed that children who are ego involved see a different value to sports than do those who are task involved. Youth who are high in task orientation are more likely to believe that sports should enhance self-esteem and sports ethos, promote personal mastery, and foster behaviors that make players into respectful and productive citizens in society at large. In short, task-oriented children subscribe to the kinds of prosocial consequences parents hope their children will attain from being involved in sports, such as good sportsmanship and team ethos. Ego-involved children are less likely to adopt those values. When children become ego involved in their performance, they miss just those aspects of sports that parents value the most.

There are further consequences of being ego involved versus task involved for children's behavior. These are most pronounced when things don't turn out well. Ego-involved children will be dejected and will feel bad about themselves when things don't go well; their motivation to pursue the sport, at least for a period of time, will diminish. Task-involved children are less likely to get down on themselves. After a failure, they are more likely to persist and to try again. Parents hope their children will learn to persevere, value teamwork, and accept the ups and downs of competition through sports. An ego-involved orientation is antithetical to these goals. Furthermore, children's motivation can determine whether or not they stick with their sport. Pelletier, Fortier, Vallerand, Tuson, Brière, and Blais (1996) measured competitive swimmers who were intrinsically motivated—were doing it for the enjoyment and pleasure—and swimmers who were extrinsically motivated—were in it for the trophies. The researchers followed the children to determine who persisted over time and who dropped out. Over the course of 1 year, children who were more intrinsically motivated were less likely to drop out. Extrinsic motivation did not have an effect. However, over 2 years' time, children who were more extrinsically motivated were more likely to drop out. Thus, engaging in activities for extrinsic rewards can take one only so far.

When it comes to sports, parents have a long list of goals for their children. First, they can certainly hope to facilitate children's intrinsic motivation. They can hope that children retain their love of the game. Second, especially as children move up the sports pyramid, a goal that parents can have for their children is to maintain a task orientation rather than an ego orientation. In this way the children can benefit from what sports involvement has to offer: camaraderie, teamwork, and good sportsmanship. Do parents make a difference in how children approach and experience sports and whether these goals are likely to be attained?

PARENTS AS SOCIALIZERS
OF CHILDREN'S SPORTS PARTICIPATION

If 20 million children are involved in sports, a staggering number of parents are finding themselves in the roles of chauffeur, coach, fan, nutritionist, physical therapist, and fundraiser. The growth in the last 20 years of youth sports has created a new phenomenon, which some refer to as the *athletic family* (Hellstedt, Rooks, & Watson, 1988). According to Hellstedt et al. (1988), a family social system has emerged that centers on the sport involvement of the children. In this system the family's time, money, and emotional energies are expended on children's sporting activities. If you grew up in such a family or are currently part of one, you know that the term *athletic family* is not an exaggeration.

There is no doubt that parents play a key role in children initiating participation in sports and in continuing that participation. Family involvement can facilitate children's participation in a number of ways. Families can provide encouragement or discouragement either verbally or symbolically. They provide the needed resources to participate, from the signing up, to the provision of transportation to the practicing of skills at home. They can also serve as models by participating themselves in sporting activities. There is clear evidence that such involvement makes a difference. One study (Brown, Frankel, & Fennell, 1989) looked at the continuity of high school girls' participation in sports. The authors asked girls how much encouragement and support their parents provided, how much the parents themselves participated in sports, and how appropriate they believed their parents felt it was for girls to participate in sports. Each of these factors contributed to girls continuing in their sports. Girls who continued their participation saw their parents as providing more encouragement and more support than did girls who did not continue. Girls who stayed with the sport were also more likely to report that their parents viewed sport as an appropriate type of activity for girls. Indeed, their parents increased their support as they grew older. These mothers and fathers were also involved in sports themselves. In a study of Israeli athletes, Melnick, Dunkelman, and Mashiach (1981) demonstrated that parents of sport-gifted children held high expectations for their children's performance and offered more encouragement for sport participation than did parents of a group of nonathletic children.

Can parents be too involved in their children's sports activities? One extreme of involvement is when the parent is coach. Is there any evidence that this can have a negative effect on children? H. Barber et al. (1999) investigated the effect of parent coaches on children's motivation for participation and competitive anxiety. Parent-coached and nonparent-coached children did not differ in reasons why they were participating or in their levels of anxiety. These results, and the positive findings for involvement, suggest that it is not high levels of involvement that are negative or lead to feelings of pressure and anxiety in children but, more likely, *how* the parents get involved and their styles of interacting with their children around sports. I now discuss this issue more specifically.

There is concern among sports psychologists about how much pressure children experience. Parental pressure has been the target of research in this area. This pressure has been defined as the amount of motivational influence that the parent exerts on the child athlete to compete in sports, perform at a certain level, and continue sport participation. There is concern that excessive parental pressure may result in anxiety and parent–child conflict, which will subsequently result in burnout and eventual withdrawal from the competitive environment. Hellstedt (1990) examined the amount of pressure exerted by parents on children aged 13 and under who were involved in competitive ski racing. Skiing is an interesting sport to investigate because it is one in which parents and children are likely to be involved concurrently. A majority of children (72.8%) in this study rated their parents as either a source of moderate or forceful pressure to compete and not to withdraw. A number of athletes (26%) felt their parents "forced" them to compete. It is interesting that most (50%) of the children felt very pleased with their parents' attitudes, whereas the rest felt either neutral (26%) or unhappy (24%). Most important, children's reaction to their parents' involvement was related to excessive parental pressure. The children who claimed the most pressure were most likely to report a negative reaction to their parents' attitudes and behavior.

Why do parents push children in sports? Many of the same arguments for academics apply to sports as well. It is quite likely that parents are easily hooked into getting ego involved in their children's athletic performance. First, parents often set their sights very high for their children's sports achievements. In a study of fathers' career expectations for their hockey-playing sons, Berlage (1981) found that fathers of 11- to 12-year-old hockey players have pronounced aspirations for their child continuing in sport. Most of the fathers hoped their sons would play hockey in high school and college, and almost all fathers felt that continued participation would help sons' careers. The reality is quite a contrast: Only 1 of every 4 youth league stars ever end up becoming stars in high school—just a few years later. The odds of a top high school player making the professional ranks in any sport are literally hundreds of thousands to 1 (Wolff, 1997).

When my daughter joined a competitive swim team, the coach gave parents a dose of reality at the very first meeting. He let us know that only a few of the children on the team would make a high school team and that none of the swimmers would make the Olympics. After he drilled this into our heads we spent the rest of the meeting discussing other goals we had for our children's participation in sports. I, personally, found this meeting extremely helpful and remember it often when Allison races well and I start to daydream about the possibilities. I believe that this kind of talk is crucial because, when parents have too much riding on sports outcomes, getting hooked is a likely outcome.

A second reason it is easy to get caught up is simply the competitive nature of the sports setting. As I argued earlier in the book, parents are invested in their children doing well and, when the environment is competitive, and they feel that their child's well-being has been threatened—whether it be a real or symbolic threat—the parent is motivated to decrease the threat. The visceral reactions we, as parents, have to seeing our children threatened evoke controlling behavior.

Also, just as I argued earlier, when parents become ego involved in children's performance they are more likely to become controlling. The yelling from the sidelines, the frustration with disappointing results, the push to perform, are all likely reactions to parents' ego involvement. In the abstract, most parents are committed to a noncompetitive philosophy. If one asks most parents what is important about sports, they will cite the camaraderie, the opportunity to develop sportsmanship, and the team ethos. In conversations off the field, parents tell their children to do their best and stress that it is how you play the game, and not whether you win, that counts. However, this rhetoric is quite at odds with parents' on the field behaviors. "Who won?" is usually the first question a parent asks when the child walks in the door from a game.

Of course, the final step in this process is the effect that parental ego involvement and controlling behavior have on children. As we have clearly seen, controlling behavior undermines children's intrinsic motivation, and it is associated with children being oriented to their performance rather than to learning. It is likely that, within the sport domain, controlling parental styles are associated with children developing ego orientations toward sports. As I argued earlier, these are antithetical to the goals that most parents have for their children. Controlling behavior can also lead to children losing their love of the game. With this in mind, I offer the following suggestions to parents.

1. *Be involved.* Research suggests that, when parents are involved, children are more likely to participate, and continue, in sports. Parents can take a variety of roles, from signing their children up for various sports, to providing encouragement and support on and off the field, to serving as team coach or manager.

2. *Monitor your reactions.* It may be helpful for parents to reflect on their goals for their children's participation in sports. Are they realistic? Are some at odds with others? The goals that center on performance are likely to be at odds with the ones that center on sportsmanship and love of the game.

3. *Prioritize and analyze goals.* Parents can put the emphasis on whether the child had fun, not on who won. Emphasizing winning facilitates an external focus for the activity and undermines children's intrinsic motivation.

4. *Decrease pressure and controlling strategies.* Children are attuned to subtle pressure from parents, such as guilt-inducing statements ("Why did you play so badly? Don't you care how I feel?"). They are also sensitive to the more overt pressures, such as rewards for attending or performing well, as well as screams from the sidelines at the child, the coach, or the referee.

5. *Increase choice.* One study showed that adults who were given a choice about which activities to include in their health fitness program attended the activities more regularly than those who were given no choice (Thompson & Wankel, 1980). Particularly for the less enjoyable aspects of sports activities, such as training to get in shape, children can be given a choice as to which activities to pursue and when.

6. *Monitor the role of others in children's sports.* Although parents can provide an autonomy supportive atmosphere for their children, there are others whose attitudes and behaviors affect children's motivation. Coaches clearly differ in their ideas about how to encourage their teams. Vince Lombardi, one of football's best-known coaches, once said: "Winning is not the most important thing. It's the only thing." This attitude seems to embody the ap-

proach of many coaches of youth teams. In the town where I live the teams are not supposed to keep score when the children are in their first few years of competitive sports—say, until age 11. However, there are clear differences in whether various coaches adhere to this rule. Some follow the rule religiously, responding to children's questions about the score with a message indicating that the numbers didn't matter. Others clearly know the scores and tell parents who ask—without stressing the actual score. At least one coach brought a score pad and actively computed not only the team score but also statistics on each 7-year-old player! Just as parents monitor the impact of a teacher on their child, parents must watch carefully to be sure that the coach is providing a positive sporting experience for the child.

I often think of the children my husband sees in his orthopedics practice. They have such a difficult time saying, perhaps even thinking, that they don't want to play. They simply turn to their physical pain. It may be the only out they have.

❧ **11** ❧

Conclusions

Jennifer, 10 years old, has taken dance lessons since she was 4. In the fall, she announced to her parents that she was quitting dance in favor of team sports: basketball, softball, and soccer. "All my friends are playing on these teams," she told her father. "I'm tired of feeling left out."

Her parents anticipated a number of problems with this plan. First, Jennifer was not particularly good at team sports. On top of this, she was highly sensitive to the competitive aspects of sports. In other words, her feelings were often and easily hurt. Second, Jennifer had especially liked being in the limelight at dance recitals. Team sports would not provide such a loving showcase. Third, her parents had invested a great deal of time and money in dance lessons. Jennifer was finally getting good. It seemed an inopportune time to quit.

How could they handle this? Should they force Jennifer to continue dance because they had invested so much and could easily see how much Jennifer was giving up? What was best for their daughter?

Jennifer's mother, weighing all these complex issues, talked with her daughter about the possible consequences of quitting dance. She stressed, however, that the ultimate decision was Jennifer's. Jennifer stuck to her decision. She opted for sports. Although she was by no means a star, she made great progress in handling the competition and the inevitable disappointments. Her parents supported her at events and picked up the pieces when she was upset at the end of a losing game. Jennifer learned to persevere.

In late spring, much to her parents' surprise, Jennifer announced that she would like to dance again. She might continue in a team sport or two, but not as intensely. Her parents bit their tongues. There weren't any "I told you so's."

T hings went right for Jennifer, one might suggest, because her parents did not become ego involved in their child's decision. That, however, would not be accurate for, as the parents report it, they did have a stake in the decision. Not only did they enjoy watching their daughter dance in recitals, but they also, with her best interests at heart, wanted her to feel good about herself. Dance was an avenue for enhancing her self-image. This situation turned out well not because Jennifer's parents divested themselves of their stake in Jennifer's achievements but because they acknowledged their feelings and did not impose their will on her.

Consistent with this, I do not believe that the route to decreasing parental control is for parents to free themselves of their investments in their children's performance. As I argued earlier, by virtue of our evolutionary heritage, parents are inevitably bound up with their offspring. Parents, feel their children's successes as their own, and they feel that their children's mistakes reflect on them.

What Jennifer's parents did was to acknowledge their feelings. They admitted that they were invested, and they worked hard not to act on their impulses to solve the problem for Jennifer and thereby impose their will on her. In short, they valued Jennifer's autonomy. Their commitment to autonomy supportive parenting outweighed their sense of ego involvement. In having Jennifer take responsibility for her own behavior—and endure the consequences—they had a clear sense of their ultimate goals for their child.

In my own life I often struggle to keep the faith that the autonomy support I attempt to provide my children will ultimately be helpful. However, even with my commitment, I admit that this is a struggle. When I see other parents pushing their children to take one more swim class in order to be sure they will do well at the next meet (and they win the race!), or when I see parents taking responsibility for their children's playground problems, I sometimes wonder whether my approach will ultimately serve my children well. I have to say, though, that the times I have strayed and controlled my children have never been happy ones. My misguided efforts have backfired (as in the toilet-training debacle I described earlier), or they have led to rifts in my relationship with the children—for example, when my daughter and I had a conflict over homework. I have always fortunately found that these rifts could be repaired. Talking through what happened, what my daughters' experience of the situation was, why I resorted to the techniques I did, and how we can do things better next time is always a viable possibility. This respect for the interactive process, and for children's opinions, is quite consistent with an autonomy supportive approach.

I have also found that life's lessons can be learned in the most unexpected places. Often these are venues where my children have wandered on their own. During a difficult year in school with a teacher who did not provide much structure or direction, my older daughter learned to take responsibility for things when they were not going well. When she wanted to get something done, she initiated it. She quickly developed her own leadership skills. After the fact, I can see that if I had constructed this experience for her by making sure everything had gone right, she would not have had the important experience that she ended up having.

My hope is that by reviewing in this book the literature on the effects of control on children that parents, professionals who work with parents and children, and researchers in the field will recognize the value of autonomy supportive parenting. The current zeitgeist in parent counseling, and a number of popular parenting books, such as syndicated columnist and author John Rosemund's guides to parenting, advocate an approach that entails high structure—which I endorse. However, they also promote the use of highly controlling techniques, including rewards and controlling praise.

Counseling appropriately stresses the importance of parents setting *a priori* rules, being consistent in applying these rules, and providing clear consequences for behavior. It is unfortunate that this structure is often combined with methods of enforcement that are controlling in nature. These counselors offer up star charts, rewards tied to performance, and pressure-filled tactics as effective parental tools to ensure that children follow rules. The research I discuss in this book suggests that these controlling techniques may lead to short-term changes in behavior and immediate compliance, but children will not internalize the value of the behavior. These techniques do not work in the long run.

I hope that the information presented here-in will persuade professionals that parents can maintain high standards, specify clear rules, and follow them through in a manner that respects children's viewpoints, minimizes pressure, and values children's input. Advocating this autonomy supportive approach means helping parents to provide clear rules and consequences. It also means helping them to allow their children to take responsibility for their own behavior. Children need the freedom to be able to make mistakes and to withstand the consequences of those mistakes.

I must point out that an autonomy supportive approach may be more difficult and more time-consuming for parents. It may be harder than, say, instituting a reward program. However, the long-term consequences and the positive parent–child relationship that could possibly result will ultimately lead to more satisfying outcomes.

Widespread dissatisfaction with schools has led to a back-to-basics movement. With a little investigation, however, one can see that "back to basics" is a code phrase for advocating strict controls, accountability, and a renewed emphasis on grades and tests. The actual classroom implementation means that teachers use the "old world" method of pushing more information into children's heads while those children passively take in what they're force fed. In his compelling book *The Schools Our Children Deserve* Alfie Kohn (1999) argued quite emphatically that this approach has never led to an increase in learning. Although I can certainly understand the frustration of watching American children lag behind those from other countries, the answer to the problem is unlikely to lie in an increase in many of the same controlling methods that have failed in the past. Rather, new methods that are learner centered, that facilitate children's activity, and that capitalize on children's innate curiosity, are warranted. Real school reform will be possible only when all parties involved, including—and especially—parents, accept the fact that better schools and higher standards cannot be equated with more control.

I also hope that the information in this book will persuade researchers to pay close attention to the real meaning of control. Because this concept has been used in so many contradictory ways, there has been a great deal of confusion in the literature. Although researchers who work primarily on the issue of parental control may be quite careful in their definitions of control, other researchers who tack this variable onto their studies as an extra component may not realize the enormous ramifications of how they are actually portraying parental control. For example, one study of parental monitoring might include "number of rules in the home" as a variable. This variable may be referred to as *level of parental control*. Imagine that these researchers then find that "number of rules" is associated with positive outcomes for children. The consumer of this study, if not carefully attuned to the way "control" was measured, may conclude that the study found control to be good. I have seen this happen many times. A study is cited as having found that control was positive in a particular population. When this happens, I seek out the original research, or I ask the authors for the measures they used in their study. I invariably find that the control measure was more akin to structure than to control. It is crucial for researchers who include parental control in their studies to be clear about their definitions of *control* and, in particular, whether they are interested in parents being "in control" or being "controlling."

A reader might say that the example I chose for the beginning of this chapter is one in which the stakes are not high. When Jennifer chose to drop her dance classes, there was always room for her to change her mind and for her parents to take up the issue again at any time. This situation allowed these parents to give Jennifer the responsibility for making the decision. In other cases, the ramifications of allowing children to make mistakes are more serious—too serious, I might suggest, for the good of children and parents. I believe that the structure of some of our institutions makes it almost impossible for parents to take an autonomy supportive stance, because decisions made early on can truly shape children's futures. The decision to sit out the travel soccer team at age 8, for example, can mean that the child does not have a chance to play at this level later, because the less advanced players are soon weeded out. The decision to forgo advanced algebra puts children on a track that is difficult to change.

In thinking about controlling parenting we must look at the interaction between individual psychologies, such as the parents' ego involvement in their children's performance, and the organizational structures around us. The competitive systems that characterize schools, sports, and other institutions make it difficult for parents to provide autonomy supportive parenting. Indeed, it may sometimes be important for parents and professionals to challenge those structures rather than giving in to them. For example, if the first-grade baseball league emphasizes scores, organizing parents to change this policy might be more useful than practicing every night to be sure the child is "good enough." Excessive focus on grades and standardized test scores in schools is a call for parental involvement in school policies.

The conditions surrounding families provide another complex challenge to parents' abilities to be autonomy supportive. As I discussed earlier, stress and financial worries set the stage for increased control. Even more extreme are dangerous circumstances such as gun- and drug-infested neighborhoods. Parents concerned for their children's lives feel forced to increase their levels of control because they see the stakes as simply too high. The conundrum, however, as we saw earlier, is that such practices undermine motivation and self-regulation. Self-regulation is as important—indeed, even more important—for children in dangerous situations as it is for children in safer environments. The prevalence of conditions that prohibit autonomy support is not just an individual but also a societal problem.

What is at stake? A great deal. In the first several chapters, I discussed how undermining control can be for children. Controlling parenting has been associated with lower levels of intrinsic motivation, less internalization of values and morals, poorer self-regulation, and higher levels of negative self-related affects. These issues relate not only to children's development and well-being but also to their success as happy, functioning adults during the course of their lives.

We already know that controlling parenting is associated with a poorer adjustment to junior high school. In recent studies conducted in my laboratory, my colleagues and I have shown that controlling parenting has ramifications for how young adults make the transition into the world of work. Young adults who perceive their parents as controlling are more external and less autonomous in their reasons for pursuing their careers than are those who describe their parents as more autonomy supportive (Jacob, 2000). More autonomous regulation of the career decision-making process is in turn associated with less anxiety and more satisfaction about the career process. Thus, the autonomy support provided by parents has definite implications for the adolescents and young adults they are shaping.

At the beginning of this book I stressed that my approach was not to pathologize parents who control their children but to understand the conditions and psychological states that result in where parents fall on the continuum between autonomy supportive and controlling. Nonetheless, the well-being of children who have been frequent recipients of controlling behavior is at risk. Alice Miller (1981) aptly described the experience of patients who come into her office and, although surrounded by the trappings of a good life and success, feel empty inside. They feel that their accomplishments are not their own. Could this be the extreme result of controlling parenting? When children go through the motions, complying with adult directives and contingencies, even the positive outcomes they accrue—good grades, trophies, and so on—do not facilitate a positive self-feeling. Only when the person feels a sense of ownership of his or her actions can positive experiences translate into healthy self-esteem and well-being. The goal of parenting for positive self-esteem is not necessarily to ensure that things go right. Ultimately it doesn't matter if the child has one more trophy on the shelf. What parents must do is to create conditions under which children can take pleasure in their own choices and accomplishments because they are theirs.

I end with the perspective of Hannah Diamond, a young girl struggling to grow up in New York in 1937. Hannah's experience is wonderfully captured in the children's book *Love From Your Friend Hannah*, by Mindy Warshaw Skolsky. In it, Hannah writes a letter to her grandmother, thanking her for saying "We like you just the way you are." Hannah goes on to explain: "The reason I like it is that grown-ups hardly ever say that to children. Mostly grown-ups tell us they would like us to make improvements. Just the way we are is usually not good enough" (p. 126).

This book is dedicated to helping parents become people who can help children grow. The message we should give our children is that just the way they are is indeed good enough.

References

Achenbach, T. M. (1991). *Manual for the youth self report and 1991 profile*. Burlington, VT: University Associates in Psychiatry.

Adorno, T., Frenkel-Brunswik, E., Levinson, D., & Sanford, N. (1950). *The authoritarian personality*. New York: Harper.

Ainsworth, M. D. S., Blehar, M. C., Waters, E., & Wall, S. (1978). *Patterns of attachment*. Hillsdale, NJ: Lawrence Erlbaum Associates.

Alderman, R. B., & Wood, N. L. (1976). An analysis of incentive motivation in young Canadian athletes. *Canadian Journal of Applied Sports Sciences, 1*, 169–176.

Amabile, T. M. (1979). Effects of external evaluation on artistic creativity. *Journal of Personality and Social Psychology, 37*, 221–233.

Amabile, T. (1983). *The social psychology of creativity*. New York: Springer-Verlag.

American Psychiatric Association. (1987). Diagnostic and statistical manual of mental disorders (3rd ed., rev.). Washington, DC: Author.

Anderson, C. A., Hinshaw, S. P., & Simmel, C. (1994). Mother–child interactions in ADHD and comparison boys: Relationships with overt and covert externalizing behavior. *Journal of Abnormal Child Psychology, 22*, 247–266.

Anderson, K. E., Lytton, H., & Romney, D. (1986). Mothers' interactions with normal and conduct disordered boys: Who affects whom? *Developmental Psychology, 22*, 604–609.

Assor, A., Roth, G., & Deci, E. (1999). *The emotional costs of memories of conditioned parental regard: A self-determination analysis*. Unpublished manuscript, Ben Gurion University, Beer Sheva, Israel.

Avery, R. R., & Ryan, R. M. (1988). Object relations and ego development: Comparison and correlates in middle childhood. *Journal of Personality, 56*, 547–569.

Baldwin, A. L. (1948). Socialization and the parent–child relationship. *Child Development, 19*, 127–137.

Baldwin, A. L. (1955). *Behavior and development in childhood*. New York: Dryden.

Baldwin, A. L., Baldwin, C., & Cole, R. E. (1990). Stress-resistant families and stress-resistant children. In J. Rolf, A. S. Masten, D. Cicchetti, K. H. Nuechterlein, & S.

Weintrab (Eds.), *Risk and protective factors in the development of psychopathology* (pp. 257–280). New York: Cambridge University Press.

Bandura, M., & Dweck, C. S. (1985). *The relationship of conceptions of intelligence and achievement goals to achievement-related cognition, affect, and behavior.* Unpublished manuscript, Harvard University.

Barber, B. K. (1996). Parental psychological control: Revisiting a neglected construct. *Child Development, 67,* 3296–3319.

Barber, B. K., Olsen, J. E., & Shagle, S. C. (1994). Associations between parental psychological and behavioral control and youth internalized and externalized behaviors. *Child Development, 65,* 1120–1136.

Barber, H., Sukhi, H., & White, S. A. (1999). The influence of parent-coaches on participant motivation and competitive anxiety in youth sport participants. *Journal of Sport Behavior, 22,* 162–176.

Barkley, R. A. (1985). The family interactions of hyperactive children: Precursors to aggressive behavior? In D. Routh & M. Wolraich (Eds.), *Advances in behavioral pediatrics* (pp. 117–150). Greenwich, CT: JAI.

Barkow, J. H. (1980). Prestige and self-esteem: A biosocial interpretation. In D. R. Omark, F. F. Strayer, & D. G. Freedman (Eds.), *Dominance relations: An ethological view of human conflict and social interaction* (pp. 319–332). New York: Garland.

Bates, J. E. (1980). The concept of difficult temperament. *Merrill–Palmer Quarterly, 26,* 299–320.

Baumrind, D. (1965). Parental control and parental love. *Children, 12,* 230–234.

Baumrind, D. (1967). Child care practices anteceding three patterns of preschool behavior. *Genetic Psychology Monographs, 75,* 43–88.

Baumrind, D. (1977, April). *Socialization determinants of personal agency.* Paper presented at the biennial meeting of the Society for Child Development, New Orleans, LA.

Baumrind, D. (1983). Rejoinder to Lewis's reinterpretation of parental firm control effects: Are authoritative families really harmonious? *Psychological Bulletin, 94,* 132–142.

Baumrind, D. (1991a). Parenting styles and adolescent development. In R. M. Lerner, A. C. Peterson, & J. Brooks-Gun (Eds.), *Encyclopedia of adolescence* (pp. 758–772). New York: Garland.

Baumrind, D. (1991b). The influence of parenting style on adolescent competence and substance use. *Journal of Early Adolescence, 11,* 56–95.

Baumrind, D. (1996). The discipline controversy revisited. *Family Relations, 45,* 405–414.

Baumrind, D., & Black, A. E. (1967). Socialization practices associated with dimensions of competence in preschool boys and girls. *Child Development, 38,* 291–327.

Beavers, W. R., & Voeller, M. N. (1983). Family models: Comparing and contrasting the Olson circumplex model with the Beavers systems model. *Family Process, 22,* 85–98.

Becker, W. C. (1964). Consequences of different kinds of parental discipline. In M. L. Hoffman & L. W. Hoffman (Eds.), *Review of child development research* (Vol. 1, pp. 169–208). New York: Russell Sage Foundation.

Bell, R. Q. (1968). A reinterpretation of the direction of effects in studies of socialization. *Psychological Review, 75,* 81–95.

Benjet, C. (1994). *The impact of parent involvement on children's motivation and school performance.* Unpublished master's thesis, Clark University, Worcester, MA.

Berlage, G. (1981, April). *Fathers' career aspirations for sons in competitive ice hockey programs*. Paper presented at the regional symposium of the International Committee for the Sociology of Sport, Vancouver, British Columbia, Canada.

Block, J. H. (1981). *The childrearing practices report (CRPR): A set of Q items for the description of parental socialization attitudes and values*. Unpublished manuscript, Institute of Human Development, University of California, Berkeley.

Blos, P. (1962). *On adolescence: A psychoanalytic interpretation*. Glencoe, IL: Free Press.

Boggiano, A. K., Barrett, M., Weiher, A. W., McClelland, G. H., & Lusk, C. M. (1987). Use of the maximal-operant principle to motivate children's intrinsic interest. *Journal of Personality and Social Psychology, 53,* 866–879.

Bowlby, J. (1969). *Attachment*. New York: Basic Books.

Brazelton, T. B., Koslowski, B., & Main, M. (1974). The origins of reciprocity: The early mother–infant interaction. In M. Lewis & L. A. Rosenblum (Eds.), *The effects of the infant on its caregiver* (pp. 49–76). New York: Wiley.

Brehm, J. W. (1966). *A theory of psychological reactance*. New York: Academic.

Bronfenbrenner, U. (1986). Ecology of the family as a context for human development. *Developmental Psychology, 22,* 723–742.

Brown, B. A. (1985). Factors influencing the process of withdrawal by female adolescents from the role of competitive age group swimmers. *Sociology of Sport Journal, 2,* 111–129.

Brown, B. A., Frankel, B. G., & Fennell, M. P. (1989). Hugs or shrugs: Parental and peer influence on continuity of involvement in sport by female adolescents. *Sex Roles, 20,* 397–412.

Buss, A. H., & Plomin, R. (1984). *A temperament theory of personality development*. New York: Wiley.

Buss, D. M. (1981). Predicting parent-child interaction from child's activity level. *Developmental Psychology, 17,* 59–65.

Cameron, J., & Pierce, W. D. (1994). Reinforcement, reward, and intrinsic motivation: A meta-analysis. *Review of Educational Research, 64,* 363–423.

Carson, B. A. (1988, April). *Advice of childrearing manuals on the use of physical punishment*. Paper presented at the Third International Conference of Family Violence Researchers, Durham, NH.

Chao, R. K. (1994). Beyond parental control and authoritarian parenting style: Understanding Chinese parenting through the cultural notion of training. *Child Development, 65,* 1111–1119.

Chapin, S. L. (1989). *Family interaction style and self-system processes in adolescents: A theoretical model and empirical investigation*. Unpublished doctoral dissertation, University of Rochester, Rochester, NY.

Chapman, M., & Zahn-Waxler, C. (1982). Young children's compliance and noncompliance to parental discipline in a natural setting. *International Journal of Behavioral Development, 5,* 81–94.

Chen, X., Dong, Q., & Zhou, H. (1997). Authoritative and authoritarian parenting practices and social and school performance in Chinese children. *International Journal of Behavioral Development, 21,* 855–873.

Chirkov, V. I., & Ryan, R. M. (2001). Parent and teacher autonomy support in Russian and U.S. adolescents: Common effects on well-being and academic motivation. *Journal of Cross-Cultural Psychology, 32,* 618–635.

Chiu, L. H. (1987). Child-rearing attitudes of Chinese, Chinese-American, and Anglo-American mothers. *International Journal of Psychology, 22,* 409–419.

Cohn, D. A. (1990). Child-mother attachment of six-year-olds and social competence at school. *Child Development, 61,* 151–162.

Conger, R. D., McCarty, J. A., Yang, R. K., Lahey, B. B., & Kropp, J. P. (1984). Perception of child, childrearing values, and emotional distress as mediating links between environmental stressors and observed maternal behavior. *Child Development, 55,* 2234–2247.

Conger, R. D., Patterson, G. R., & Ge, X. (1995). It takes two to replicate: A mediational model for the impact of parents' stress on adolescent adjustment. *Child Development, 66,* 80–97.

Coopersmith, S. (1967). *The antecedents of self-esteem.* San Francisco: Freeman.

Cordova, D. I., & Lepper, M. R. (1996). Intrinsic motivation and the process of learning: Beneficial effects of contextualization, personalization, and choice. *Journal of Educational Psychology, 88,* 715–730.

Crouter, A. C., MacDermid, S. M., McHale, S. M., & Perry-Jenkins, M. (1990). Parental monitoring and perceptions of children's school performance and conduct in dual- and single-earner families. *Developmental Psychology, 26,* 649–657.

Csikszentmihalyi, M. (1990). *Flow: The psychology of optimal experience.* New York: Harper & Row.

Darling, N., & Steinberg, L. (1993). Parenting style as context: An integrative model. *Psychological Bulletin, 113,* 487–496.

Dawber, T., & Kuczynski, L. (1999). The question of ownness: The influence of relationship context on parental socialization strategies. *Journal of Social and Personal Relationships, 16,* 475–493.

Dawkins, R. (1976). *The selfish gene.* New York: Oxford University Press.

deCharms, R. (1968). *Personal causation: The internal affective determinants of behavior.* New York: Academic.

Deci, E. L. (1971). Effects of externally mediated rewards on intrinsic motivation. *Journal of Personality and Social Psychology, 18,* 105–115.

Deci, E. L. (1975). *Intrinsic motivation.* New York: Plenum.

Deci, E. L., Betley, G., Kahle, J., Abrams, L., & Porac, J. (1981). When trying to win: Competition and intrinsic motivation. *Personality and Social Psychology Bulletin, 7,* 79–83.

Deci, E. L., & Cascio, W. F. (1972, April). *Changes in intrinsic motivation as a function of negative feedback and threats.* Paper presented at the annual meeting of the Eastern Psychological Association, Boston, MA.

Deci, E. L., Connell, J. P., & Ryan, R. M. (1989). Self-determination in a work organization. *Journal of Applied Psychology, 74,* 580–590.

Deci, E. L., & Driver, R. E., Hotchkiss, L., Robbins, R. J., & Wilson, I. M. (1993). The relations of mothers' controlling vocalizations to children's intrinsic motivation. *Journal of Experimental Child Psychology, 55,* 151–162.

Deci, E. L., Eghrari, H., Patrick, B. C., & Leone, D. R. (1994). Facilitating internalization: The self-determination theory perspective. *Journal of Personality, 62,* 119–142.

Deci, E. L., Koestner, R., & Ryan, R. M. (1999). A meta-analytic review of experiments examining the effects of extrinsic rewards on intrinsic motivation. *Psychological Bulletin, 125,* 627–668.

Deci, E. L., Nezlek , J., & Sheinman, L. (1981). Characteristics of rewarder and intrinsic motivation of rewardee. *Journal of Personality and Social Psychology, 40*, 1–10.

Deci, E. L., & Ryan, R. M. (1985a). The General Causality Orientations Scale: Self determination in personality. *Journal of Research in Personality, 19*, 109–134.

Deci, E. L., & Ryan, R. M. (1985b). *Intrinsic motivation and self-regulation in human behavior.* New York: Plenum.

Deci, E. L., Spiegel, N. H., Ryan, R. M., Koestner, R., & Kauffman, M. (1982). The effects of performance standards on teaching styles: The behavior of controlling teachers. *Journal of Educational Psychology, 74*, 852–859.

Dornbusch, S. M., Ritter, P. L., Leiderman, P. H., Roberts, D. F., & Fraleigh, M. J. (1987). The relation of parenting style to adolescent school performance. *Child Development, 58*, 1244–1257.

Doty, R. M., Peterson, B. E., & Winter, D. G. (1991). Threat and authoritarianism in the United States, 1978–1987. *Journal of Personality and Social Psychology, 61*, 629–640.

Duda, J. L. (1992). Motivation in sport settings: A goal perspective approach. In G. C. Roberts (Ed.), *Motivation in sport and exercise* (pp. 59–92). Champaign, IL: Human Kinetics.

Duncan, G. J. (1991). The economic environment of childhood. In A. C. Huston (Ed.), *Children in poverty* (pp. 23–50). New York: Cambridge University Press.

Dweck, C. S., & Leggett, E. L. (1988). A social-cognitive approach to motivation and personality. *Psychological Review, 95*, 256–273.

Eccles, J. S., & Midgley, C. (1988). Stage/environment fit: Developmentally appropriate classrooms for young adolescents. In R. E. Ames & C. Ames (Eds.), *Research on motivation in education* (Vol. 3, pp. 139–186). New York: Academic.

Eccles, J. S., Midgley, C., Wigfield, A., Buchanan, C. M., Reuman, D., Flanagan, C., & Mac Iver, D. (1993). Development during adolescence: The impact of stage–environment fit on adolescents' experiences in schools and families. *American Psychologist, 48*, 90–101.

Eisenberg, N. (1986). *Altruistic emotion, cognition and behavior.* Hillsdale, NJ: Lawrence Erlbaum Associates.

Eisenberger, R., & Cameron, J. (1996). Detrimental effects of reward: Reality or myth? *American Psychologist, 51*, 1153–1166.

Epstein, J. L. (1983). Longitudinal effects of family–school–person interactions on student outcomes. In A. Kerckhoff (Ed.), *Research in sociology of education and socialization* (Vol. 4, pp. 101–128). Greenwich, CT: JAI.

Farson, R. E. (1963). Praise reappraised. *Harvard Business Review, 41*, 61–66.

Feingold, B. D., & Mahoney, M. J. (1975). Reinforcement effects on intrinsic interest: Undermining the overjustification hypothesis. *Behavior Therapy, 6*, 357–377.

Feldman, S., & Stenner, K. (1997). Perceived threat and authoritarianism. *Political Psychology, 18*, 741–770.

Flanagan, C. (1985, April). *The relationship of family environments in early adolescence and intrinsic motivation in the classroom.* Paper presented at the annual meeting of the American Educational Research Association, San Francisco.

Fuligni, A. J., & Eccles, J. S. (1990). *Early adolescent peer orientation and parent–child relationships.* Unpublished manuscript, Institute for Social Research, University of Michigan.

Fuligni, A. J., Tseng, V., & Lam, M. (1999). Attitudes toward family obligations among American adolescents with Asian, Latin American, & European backgrounds. *Child Development, 70*, 1030–1044.

Ge, X., Conger, R. D., & Stewart, M. A. (1996). The developmental interface between nature and nurture: A mutual influence model of child antisocial behavior and parent behaviors. *Developmental Psychology, 32,* 574–584.

Gill, D. L., Gross, J., & Huddleston, S. (1983). Participation motivation in youth sports. *International Journal of Sport Psychology, 14,* 1–14.

Ginott, H. (1965). *Between parent and child.* New York: Macmillan.

Greenberg, M. T., Kusche, C. A., & Speltz, M. (1991). Emotional regulation, self-control, and psychopathology: The role of relationships in early childhood. In D. Cicchetti & S. L. Toth (Eds.), *Internalizing and externalizing expressions of dysfunction* (pp. 21–56). Hillsdale, NJ: Lawrence Erlbaum Associates.

Grolnick, W. S. (1987). *Parental styles associated with children's school-related self-regulation and competence: A motivational perspective.* Doctoral dissertation, University of Rochester, Rochester, NY.

Grolnick, W. S., Benjet, C., Kurowski, C., & Apostoleris, N. (1997). Predictors of parent involvement in children's schooling. *Journal of Educational Psychology, 89,* 1–11.

Grolnick, W. S., Bridges, L. J., & Connell, J. P. (1996). Emotion regulation in two-year-olds: Strategies and emotional expression in four contexts. *Child Development, 67,* 928–941.

Grolnick, W. S., Frodi, A., & Bridges, L. J. (1984). Maternal control style and the mastery motivation of one-year-olds. *Infant Mental Health Journal, 5,* 72–82.

Grolnick, W. S., Gehl, K., & Manzo, C. (1997, April). *Longitudinal effects of parent involvement and autonomy support on children's motivational resources and school performance.* Paper presented at the Biennial Meeting of the Society for Research on Child Development, Washington, DC.

Grolnick, W. S., & Gurland, S. T. (1999, April). *Women and mothering: Retrospect and prospect.* Paper presented at Interiors: Retrospect and Prospect in the Psychological Study of Families, Clark University, Worcester, MA.

Grolnick, W. S., Gurland, S. T., DeCourcey, W., & Jacob, K. (2002). Antecedents and consequences of mother's autonomy support: An experimental investigation. *Developmental Psychology, 38,* 143–155.

Grolnick, W. S., Kurowski, C. O., Dunlap, K., & Hevey, C. (2000). Parental resources and the transition to junior high. *Journal of Research on Adolescence, 10,* 465–480.

Grolnick, W. S., & Ryan, R. M. (1987). Autonomy in children's learning: An experimental and individual difference investigation. *Journal of Personality and Social Psychology, 52,* 890–898.

Grolnick, W. S., & Ryan, R. M. (1989). Parent styles associated with children's self-regulation and competence in school. *Journal of Educational Psychology, 81,* 143–154.

Grolnick, W. S., & Ryan, R. M. (1990). Self-perceptions, motivation, and adjustment in children with learning disabilities: A multiple group comparison study. *Journal of Learning Disabilities, 23,* 177–184.

Grolnick, W. S., Deci, E. L., & Ryan, R. M. (1991). The inner resources for school achievement: Motivational mediators of children's perceptions of their parents. *Journal of Educational Psychology, 83,* 508–517.

Grolnick, W. S., Ryan, R. M., & Deci, E. L. (1997). Internalization within the family: The self-determination theory perspective. In J. E. Grusec & L. Kuczynski (Eds.), *Parenting and children's internalization of values* (pp. 135–161). New York: Wiley.

Grolnick, W. S., & Slowiaczek, M. (1994). Parents' involvement in children's schooling: A multidimensional conceptualization and motivational model. *Child Development, 65,* 237–252.

Grolnick, W. S., Weiss, L., McKenzie, L., & Wrightman, J. (1996). Contextual, cognitive, and adolescent factors associated with parenting in adolescence. *Journal of Youth and Adolescence, 25,* 33–54.

Gross, J. (2000, July 16). Grade-school game: Pick the teacher. *New York Times,* p. B1.

Grusec, J. E., & Goodnow, J. J. (1994). Impact of parental discipline methods on the child's internalization of values: A reconceptualization of current points of view. *Developmental Psychology, 30,* 4–19.

Grusec, J. E., & Redler, E. (1980). Attribution, reinforcement, and altruism: A developmental analysis. *Developmental Psychology, 16,* 525–634.

Gurland, S. T., & Grolnick, W. S. (2000). *Children's expectancies of adults: Effects of confirmation versus disconfirmation.* Unpublished manuscript, Clark University.

Harach, L., & Kuczynski, L. (1999, April). *Defining and constructing relationships from the perspective of parents.* Paper presented at the biennial meeting of the Society for Research in Child Development, Albuquerque, NM.

Harackiewicz, J., Manderlink, G., & Sansone, C. (1984). Rewarding pinball wizardry: The effects of evaluation on intrinsic interest. *Journal of Personality and Social Psychology, 47,* 287–300.

Harkness, S., & Super, C. M. (1997). An infant's three Rs. *Natural History, 106,* 45.

Harlow, H. F. (1958). The nature of love. *American Psychologist, 13,* 673–685.

Harlow, H. F., Harlow, M. K., & Meyer, D. R. (1950). Learning motivated by a manipulation drive. *Journal of Experimental Psychology, 40,* 228–234.

Hatfield, J. S., Ferguson, L. R., & Alpert, R. (1967). Mother-child interaction and the socialization process. *Child Development, 38,* 365–414.

Heider, F. (1958). *The psychology of interpersonal relations.* New York: Wiley.

Hellstedt, J. C. (1990). Early adolescent perceptions of parental pressure in the sport environment. *Journal of Sport Behavior, 13,* 135–144.

Hellstedt, J., Rooks, D., & Watson, D. (1988). *On the sidelines: Decisions, skills, and training in youth sport.* Amherst, MA: Human Resource Development.

Hess, R. D., & Shipman, V. C. (1965). Early experience and the socialization of cognitive modes in children. *Child Development, 36,* 869–886.

Hinshaw, S. P., Zupan, B. A., Simmel, C., Nigg, J. T., & Melnick, S. (1997). Peer status in boys with and without attention-deficit hyperactivity disorder: Predictions from overt and covert antisocial behavior, social isolation, and authoritative parenting. *Child Development, 68,* 880–896.

Hoffman, M. L. (1960). Power assertion by the parent and its impact on the child. *Child Development, 31,* 129–143.

Hoffman, M. L. (1970). Moral development. In P. H. Mussen (Ed.), *Carmichael's manual of child psychology* (Vol. 2, pp. 261–359). New York: Wiley.

Hofstede, G. (1991). *Cultures and organizations: Software of the mind.* London: McGraw Hill.

Hunt, D. E. (1975). Person–environment interaction: A challenge found wanting before it was tried. *Review of Educational Research, 45,* 209–230.

Ispa, J. M. (1995). Ideas about infant and toddler care among Russian child care teachers, mothers, and University students. *Early Childhood Research Quarterly, 10,* 359–379.

Jacob, K. (2000). *A self-determination theory analysis of the transition into the world of work*. Unpublished master's thesis, Clark University.

Jelsma, B. M. (1982). *Adult control behaviors: The interaction between orientation toward control in women and activity level of children*. Unpublished doctoral dissertation, University of Rochester.

Johnston, C. (1996). Parent characteristics and parent–child interactions in families of nonproblem children and ADHD children with higher and lower levels of oppositional-defiant behavior. *Journal of Abnormal Child Psychology, 24*, 85–105.

Kadushin, A., & Martin, J. A. (1981). *Child abuse: An interactional event*. New York: Columbia University Press.

Kamins, M. L., & Dweck, C. S. (1999). Person versus process praise and criticism: Implications for contingent self-worth and coping. *Developmental Psychology, 35*, 835–847.

Kanouse, D. E., Gumpert, P., & Canavan-Gumpert, D. (1981). The semantics of praise. In J. H. Harvey, W. Ickes, & R. F. Kidd (Eds.), *New directions in attribution research* (Vol. 3, pp. 97–115). Hillsdale, NJ: Lawrence Erlbaum Associates.

Karniol, R., & Ross, M. (1976). The development of causal attributions in social perception. *Journal of Personality and Social Psychology, 34*, 455–464.

Kasser, T. (2002). Sketches for a self-determination theory of values. In E. L. Deci & R. M. Ryan (Eds.), *Handbook of self-determination theory* (pp. 123–140). Rochester, NY: University of Rochester Press.

Kast, A., & Connor, K. (1988). Sex and age differences in response to informational and controlling feedback. *Personality and Social Psychology Bulletin, 14*, 514–523.

Kelley, M. L. (1988). *Conceptions of parenting in low-income, Black urban mothers*. Unpublished doctoral dissertation, University of Houston.

Kelley, M. L., Power, T. G., & Wimbush, D. D. (1992). Determinants of disciplinary practices in low-income Black mothers. *Child Development, 63*, 573–582.

Kelley, M., Sanchez-Hucles, J., & Walker, R. R. (1993). Correlates of disciplinary practices in working to middle-class African-American mothers. *Merrill–Palmer Quarterly, 39*, 252–264.

Kelman, H. C. (1961). Processes of attitude change. *Public Opinion Quarterly, 25*, 57–78.

Kersey, B., & Protinsky, H. (1987). Family structure variables and psychological adjustment in adolescence. *International Journal of Family Psychiatry, 8*, 89–98.

Kochanska, G. (1995). Children's temperament, mothers' discipline, and security of attachment: Multiple pathways to emerging internalization. *Child Development, 66*, 597–615.

Kochanska, G. (1997). Mutually responsive orientation between mothers and their young children: Implications for early socialization. *Child Development, 68*, 94–112.

Kochanska, G., & Aksan, N. (1995). Mother-child mutually positive affect, the quality of child compliance to requests and prohibitions, and maternal control as correlates of early internalization. *Child Development, 66*, 236–254.

Kochanska, G., Aksan, N., & Koenig, A. L. (1995). A longitudinal study of the roots of preschoolers' conscience: Committed compliance and emerging internalization. *Child Development, 66*, 1752–1769.

Koestner, R., Bernieri, F., & Zuckerman, M. (1992). Self-regulation and consistency between attitudes, traits, and behaviors. *Personality and Social Psychology Bulletin, 18*, 52–59.

Koestner, R., Ryan, R. M., Bernieri, F., & Holt, K. (1984). Setting limits on children's behavior: The differential effects of controlling versus informational styles on intrinsic motivation and creativity. *Journal of Personality, 52,* 244–248.

Kohlberg, L. (1976). Moral stages and moralization: The cognitive developmental approach. In T. Lickona (Ed.), *Moral development and moral behavior: Theory, research, and social issues* (pp. 31–53). New York: Holt, Rinehart & Winston.

Kohn, A. (1998, April). Only for my kid: How privileged parents undermine school reform. *Phi Delta Kappan,* 569–577.

Kohn, A. (1999). *The schools our children deserve.* New York: Houghton Mifflin.

Kohn, M. L. (1977). *Class and conformity* (2nd ed.). Chicago: University of Chicago Press.

Kuczynski, L. (1984). Socialization goals and mother–child interaction: Strategies for long-term and short-term compliance. *Developmental Psychology, 20,* 1061–1073.

Kuczynski, L., Harach, L., & Bernardini, C. (1999). Psychology's child meets sociology's child: Agency, influence and power in parent–child relationships. *Contemporary Perspectives on Family Research, 1,* 21–52.

Labaree, D. F. (1997). *How to succeed in school without really learning: The credentials race in American education.* New Haven, CT: Yale University Press.

Lamborn, S., Dornbusch, S., & Steinberg, L. (1996). Ethnicity and community context as moderators of the relation between family decision-making and adolescent adjustment. *Child Development, 67,* 283–301.

Larzelere, R. E. (2000). Child outcomes of nonabusive and customary physical punishment by parents: An updated literature review. *Clinical Child and Family Psychology Review, 3,* 199–221.

Larzelere, R. E., Kuhn, B. R., & Johnson, B. (2000). *The intervention selection bias.* Unpublished manuscript.

Larzelere, R. E., Sather, P. R., Schneider, W. N., Larson, D. B., & Pike, P. L. (1998). Punishment enhances reasoning effectiveness as a disciplinary response to toddlers. *Journal of Marriage and the Family, 60,* 388–403.

Lee, C. L., & Bates, J. E. (1985). Mother–child interaction at age two years and perceived difficult temperament. *Child Development, 56,* 1314–1325.

Leone, C. M., & Richards, M. H. (1989). Classwork and homework in early adolescence: The ecology of achievement. *Journal of Youth and Adolescence, 18,* 531–548.

Lepper, M. R. (1973). Dissonance, self-perception and honesty in children. *Journal of Personality and Social Psychology, 25,* 65–74.

Lepper, M. R. (1983). Social-control processes and the internalization of social values: An attributional perspective. In E. T. Higgins, D. N. Ruble, & W. W. Hartup (Eds.), *Social cognition and social development* (pp. 294–330). New York: Cambridge University Press.

Lepper, M. R., & Gilovich, T. (1982). Accentuating the positive: Eliciting generalized compliance from children through activity-oriented requests. *Journal of Personality and Social Psychology, 42,* 248–259.

Lepper, M. R., & Greene, D. (1975). Turning play into work: Effects of adult surveillance and extrinsic rewards on children's intrinsic motivation. *Journal of Personality and Social Psychology, 31,* 479–486.

Lepper, M. R., Greene, D., & Nisbett, R. E. (1973). Undermining children's intrinsic interest with extrinsic rewards: A test of the "overjustification" hypothesis. *Journal of Personality and Social Psychology, 28,* 129–137.

Lewis, C. C. (1981). The effects of parental firm control: A reinterpretation of findings. *Psychological Bulletin, 90*, 547–563.

Lin, C. C., & Fu, V. R. (1990). A comparison of child-rearing practices among Chinese, immigrant Chinese, and Caucasian-American parents. *Child Development, 61*, 429–433.

Little, T. D. (1997). Mean and covariance structure (MACS) analysis of cross-cultural data: Practical and theoretical issues. *Multivariate Behavioral Research, 32*, 53–76.

Loeb, R. C., Horst, L., & Horton, P. J. (1980). Family interaction patterns associated with self-esteem in preadolescent girls and boys. *Merrill-Palmer Quarterly, 26*, 203–217.

Lollis, S., & Kuczynski, L. (1997). Beyond one-hand clapping: Seeing bidirectionality in parent-child relations. *Journal of Social and Personal Relationships, 14*, 441–461.

Longfellow, C., Zelkowitz, P., & Saunders, E. (1982). The quality of mother-child relationships. In D. Belle (Ed.), *Lives in stress: Women and depression* (pp. 163–176). Beverly Hills, CA: Sage.

Lovejoy, O. (1981, January). The origin of man. *Science, 211*, 341–350.

Luchins, A. S. (1942). Mechanization in problem solving: The effect of Einstelung. *Psychological Monographs, 54*(6, Whole No. 248).

Lytton, H. (1980). *Parent–child interaction: The socialization process observed in twin and singleton families.* New York: Plenum.

Maccoby, E. E. (1980). *Social development: Psychological growth and the parent–child relationship.* New York: Harcourt Brace.

MacDonald, K. B. (1988). *Sociobiological perspectives on human development.* New York: Springer-Verlag.

Mac Iver, D., & Reuman, D. A. (1988, April). *Decision-making in the classroom and early adolescents' valuing of mathematics.* Paper presented at the meeting of the American Educational Research Association, San Francisco.

Markus, H., & Kitayama, S. (1991). Culture and self: Implications for cognition, emotion, and motivation. *Psychological Review, 98*, 224–253.

McAuley, E., & Tammen, V. V. (1989). The effects of subjective and objective competitive outcomes on intrinsic motivation. *Journal of Sport and Exercise Psychology, 11*, 84–93.

McCartney, K., Robeson, W. W., Jordan, E., & Mouradian, V. (1991). Mothers' language with first- and second-born children: A within-family study. In K. A. Pillemer & K. McCartney (Eds.), *Parent-child relations throughout life* (pp. 125–142). Hillsdale, NJ: Lawrence Erlbaum Associates.

McGraw, K. O., & McCullers, J. C. (1979). Evidence of a detrimental effect of extrinsic incentives on breaking a mental set. *Journal of Experimental Social Psychology, 15*, 285–294.

McLoyd, V. C., Jayaratne, T. E., Ceballo, R., & Borquez, J. (1994). Unemployment and work interruption among African American single mothers: Effects on parenting and adolescent socioemotional functioning. *Child Development, 65*, 562–589.

McLoyd, V. C., & Wilson, L. (1991). The strain of living poor: Parenting, social support, and child mental health. In A. C. Huston (Ed.), *Children in poverty* (pp. 105–135). New York: Cambridge University Press.

Meissner, W. W. (1981). *Internalization in psychoanalysis.* New York: International Universities Press.

Melnick, M., Dunkelman, N., & Mashiach, A. (1981). Familial factors of sports giftedness among young Israeli athletes. *Journal of Sport Behavior, 4*, 82–94.

Michael, R. T., Fuchs, V. R., & Scott, S. R. (1980). Changes in the propensity to live alone: 1950–1976. *Demography, 17,* 39–56.

Midgely, C., & Feldlaufer, H. (1987). Students' and teachers' decision-making fit before and after the transition to junior high school. *Journal of Early Adolescence, 7,* 225–241.

Miller, A. (1981). *The drama of the gifted child.* New York: Basic Books.

Mills, R., & Rubin, K. H. (1993). Socialization factors in the development of social withdrawal. In K. H. Rubin & J. Asendorpf (Eds.), *Social withdrawal, inhibition, and shyness in childhood* (pp. 117–148). Hillsdale, NJ: Lawrence Erlbaum Associates.

Minton, C., Kagan, J., & Levine, J. A. (1971). Maternal control and obedience in two-year-olds. *Child Development, 42,* 1873–1894.

Minuchin, S. (1974). *Families and family therapy.* Cambridge, MA: Harvard University Press.

Montemayor, R. (1982). The relationship between parent–adolescent conflict and the amount of time adolescents spend alone and with parents and peers. *Child Development, 13,* 1512–1519.

Mueller, C. M., & Dweck, C. S. (1996, April). *Implicit theories of intelligence: Relation of parental beliefs to children's expectations.* Paper presented at Head Start's Third National Research Conference, Washington, DC.

Mueller, C. M., & Dweck, C. S. (1998). Praise for intelligence can undermine children's motivation and performance. *Journal of Personality and Social Psychology, 75,* 33–52.

O'Connor, T. G., Deater-Deckard, K., Fulker, D., Rutter, M., & Plomin, R. (1998). Genotype-environment correlations in late childhood and early adolescence: Antisocial behavioral problems and coercive parenting. *Developmental Psychology, 34,* 970–981.

Offer, D., Ostrov, E., & Howard, K. I. (1981). *The adolescent: A psychological self-portrait.* New York: Basic Books.

Olsen, D. H., McCubbin, H. I., Barnes, H., Larsen, A., Muxen, M., & Wilson, M. (1985). *Family inventories.* St. Paul, MN: Family Social Science, University of Minnesota.

Olsen, D. H., Sprenkle, D. H., & Russell, C. (1979). Circumplex model of marital and family systems: I. Cohesion and adaptability dimensions, family types, and clinical applications. *Family Process, 18,* 3–15.

Orlick, T. (1978). *Winning through cooperation: Competitive insanity, cooperative alternatives.* Washington, DC: Acropolis Books.

Orlick, T. D., & Mosher, R. (1978). Extrinsic awards and participant motivation in a sport related task. *International Journal of Sport Psychology, 9,* 27–39.

Parker, G., Tupling, H., & Brown, L. B. (1979). A parental bonding instrument. *British Journal of Medical Psychology, 52,* 1–10.

Parker, L., & Lepper, M. R. (1992). The effects of fantasy contexts on children's learning and motivation: Making learning more fun. *Journal of Personality and Social Psychology, 62,* 625–633.

Patterson, G. R. (1982). *Coercive family processes.* Eugene, OR: Castalia.

Patterson, G. R., & Stouthamer-Loeber, M. (1984). The correlation of family management practices and delinquency. *Child Development, 55,* 1299–1307.

Pelletier, L. G., Fortier, M. S., Vallerand, R. J., Tuson, K. M., Brière, N. M., & Blais, M. R. (1996). Toward a new measure of intrinsic motivation, extrinsic motivation, and amotivation in sports: The Sport Motivation Scale (SMS). *Journal of Sport and Exercise Psychology, 17,* 35–54.

Piuck, C. (1975). Child-rearing patterns of poverty. *American Journal of Psychotherapy, 29*, 485–502.

Plant, R., & Ryan, R. M. (1985). Intrinsic motivation and the effects of self-consciousness, self-awareness, and ego-involvement: An investigation of internally controlling styles. *Journal of Personality, 53*, 435–449.

Plomin, R., Reiss, D., Hetherington, E. M., & Howe, G. W. (1994). Nature and nurture: Genetic contributions to measures of the family environment. *Developmental Psychology, 30*, 32–43.

Pomerantz, E. M., & Eaton, M. M. (2000). Developmental differences in children's conceptions of parental control: "They love me but they make me feel incompetent." *Merrill–Palmer Quarterly, 46*, 140–167.

Pomerantz, E. M., & Eaton, M. M. (2001). Maternal intrusive support in the academic context: Transactional socialization processes. *Developmental Psychology, 37*, 174–186.

Pomerantz, E. M., & Ruble, P. N. (1998). The role of maternal control in the development of sex differences in child's self-evaluative factors. *Child Development, 69*, 458–478.

Potter-Efron, R. T. (1989). *Shame, guilt, and alcoholism: Treatment issues in clinical practice.* New York: Haworth.

Powers, S. I. (1982). *Family environments and adolescent moral development: A study of psychiatrically hospitalized and non-patient adolescents.* Unpublished doctoral dissertation, Harvard University.

Powers, S. I., Hauser, S. T., Schwartz, J., Noam, G. G., & Jacobson, A. M. (1983). Adolescent ego development and family interaction: A structural–developmental perspective. *New Directions for Child Development, 22*, 5–25.

Pulkkinen, L. (1982). Self-control and continuity from childhood to adolescence. In P. B. Baltes & O. G. Brim (Eds.), *Life-span development and behavior* (Vol. 4, pp. 63–105). New York: Academic.

Reeve, J., & Deci, E. L. (1996). Elements of the competitive situation that affect intrinsic motivation. *Personality and Social Psychology Bulletin, 22*, 24–33.

Reiss, S., & Sushinsky, L. W. (1975). Overjustification, competing responses, and the acquisition of intrinsic interest. *Journal of Personality and Social Psychology, 31*, 1116–1125.

Repetti, R. L. (1994). Short-term and long-term processes linking job stressors to father–child interaction. *Social Development, 3*, 1–15.

Repetti, R. L., & Wood, J. (1997). Effects of daily stress at work on mothers' interactions with preschoolers. *Journal of Family Psychology, 11*, 90–108.

Reynolds, A. J., Mavrogenes, N. A., Bezruczko, N., & Hageman, M. (1996). Cognitive and family support mediators of preschool effectiveness: A confirmatory analysis. *Child Development, 67*, 1119–1140.

Richters, J. E., & Waters, E. (1991). Attachment and socialization: The positive side of social influence. In M. Lewis & S. Feinman (Eds.), *Social influences and socialization in infancy* (pp. 185–213). New York: Plenum.

Roberts, G., & Kleiber, D. (1982). *The importance of perceived ability in the developing child's participation in recreation and sport. Leisure research.* Symposium conducted at the annual meeting of the National Recreation and Parks Association Annual Meeting, Louisville, KY.

Rohner, R. P. (1986). *The warmth dimension: Foundation of parental-acceptance-rejection theory.* Newbury Park, CA: Sage.

Rohner, R. P., & Pettengill, S. M. (1985). Perceived parental acceptance-rejection and parental control among Korean adolescents. *Child Development, 56,* 524–528.

Ross, M. (1975). Salience of reward and intrinsic motivation. *Journal of Personality and Social Psychology, 32,* 245–254.

Rutter, M., & Quinton, D. (1984). Long-term follow-up of women institutionalized in childhood: Factors promoting good functioning in adult life. *British Journal of Developmental Psychology, 18,* 225–234.

Ryan, R. M. (1982). Control and information in the intrapersonal sphere: An extension of cognitive evaluation theory. *Journal of Personality and Social Psychology, 43,* 450–461.

Ryan, R. M. (1995). Psychological needs and the facilitation of integrative processes. *Journal of Personality, 63,* 397–428.

Ryan, R. M., & Connell, J. P. (1989). Perceived locus of causality and internalization: Examining reasons for acting in two domains. *Journal of Personality and Social Psychology, 57,* 749–761.

Ryan, R. M., Connell, J. P., & Deci, E. L. (1985). A motivational analysis of self-determination and self-regulation in education. In C. Ames & R. E. Ames (Eds.), *Research on motivation in education: The classroom milieu* (pp. 13–51). New York: Academic.

Ryan, R. M., & Grolnick, W. S. (1986). Origins and pawns in the classroom: Self-report and projective assessments of individual differences in children's perceptions. *Journal of Personality and Social Psychology, 50,* 550–558.

Ryan, R. M., & Lynch, J. (1989). Emotional autonomy versus detachment: Revisiting the vicissitudes of adolescence and young adulthood. *Child Development, 60,* 340–356.

Ryan, R. M., Mims, V., & Koestner, R. (1983). Relation of reward contingency and interpersonal context to intrinsic motivation: A review and test using cognitive evaluation theory. *Journal of Personality and Social Psychology, 45,* 736–750.

Ryan, R. M., Stiller, J., & Lynch, J. H. (1994). Representations of relationships to teachers, parents, and friends as predictors of academic motivation and self-esteem. *Journal of Early Adolescence, 14,* 226–249.

Sales, S. M. (1972). Economic threat as a determinant of conversion rates in authoritarian and nonauthoritarian churches. *Journal of Personality and Social Psychology, 23,* 420–428.

Sales, S. M., & Friend, K. E. (1973). Success and failure as determinants of level of authoritarianism. *Behavioral Science, 18,* 163–172.

Sanders, S. (1999). *Champions are raised, not born: How my parents made me a success.* New York: Delacorte.

Schaefer, E. S. (1959). A circumplex model for maternal behavior. *Journal of Abnormal and Social Psychology, 59,* 226–235.

Schaefer, E. S. (1965a). A configural analysis of children's reports of parent behavior. *Journal of Consulting Psychology, 29,* 552–557.

Schaefer, E. S. (1965b). Children's reports of parental behavior: An inventory. *Child Development, 36,* 413–424.

Schafer, R. (1968). *Aspects of internalization.* New York: International Universities Press.

Sears, R. R., Maccoby, E. C., & Levin, H. (1957). *Patterns of child rearing.* Evanston, IL: Row, Peterson.

Sherif, M., & Cantril, H. (1947). *The psychology of ego involvements, social attitudes, and identifications.* New York: Wiley.

Silverstein, L. B. (2002). Fathers and families. In J. P. McHale & W. Grolnick (Eds.), *Retrospect and prospect in the psychological study of families* (pp. 35–64). Mahwah, NJ: Lawrence Erlbaum Associates.

Simons, R. L., & Johnson, C. (1996). Mother's parenting. In R. L. Simons (Ed.), *Understanding differences between divorced and intact families: Stress, interaction, and child outcome* (pp. 81–93). Thousand Oaks, CA: Sage.

Skolsky, M. W. (1998). *Love from your friend Hannah.* New York: DK Publishing.

Smith, M. C. (1975). Children's use of the multiple sufficient cause schema in social perception. *Journal of Personality and Social Psychology, 32,* 737–747.

Sroufe, L. A., & Fleeson, J. (1986). *Attachment and the construction of relationships.* In W. W. Hartup & Z. Rubin (Eds.), *Relationships and development* (pp. 51–71). Hillsdale, NJ: Lawrence Erlbaum Associates.

Sroufe, L. A., & Waters, E. (1977). Attachment as an organizational construct. *Child Development, 48,* 1184–1199.

Steinberg, L. (1990). Autonomy, conflict, and harmony in the family relationship. In S. Feldman & G. Elliot (Eds.), *At the threshold: The developing adolescent* (pp. 255–276). Cambridge, MA: Harvard University Press.

Steinberg, L. (1996). *Beyond the classroom.* New York: Simon & Schuster.

Steinberg, L., Elmen, J. D., & Mounts, N. S. (1989). Authoritative parenting, psychosocial maturity, and academic success among adolescents. *Child Development, 60,* 1424–1436.

Steinberg, L., Lamborn, S. D., Dornbusch, S. M., & Darling, N. (1992). Impact of parenting practices on adolescent achievement: Authoritative parenting, school involvement, and encouragement to succeed. *Child Development, 63,* 1266–1281.

Steinberg, L., Mounts, N., Lamborn, S., & Dornbusch, S. (1991). Authoritative parenting and adolescent adjustment across various ecological niches. *Journal of Research on Adolescence, 1,* 19–36.

Stevenson, D., & Baker, D. (1987). The family–school relation and the child's school performance. *Child Development, 58,* 1348–1357.

Stevenson, H. W., Lee, S., Chen, C., Stigler, J., Hsu, C. C., & Kitamura, S. (1990). Contexts of achievement: A study of American, Chinese, and Japanese children. *Monographs of the Society for Research in Child Development, 55*(1–2, Serial No. 221).

Stipek, D., & Mac Iver, D. (1989). Developmental change in children's assessment of intellectual competence. *Child Development, 60,* 521–538.

Strassberg, Z., Dodge, K. A., Petit, G. S., & Bates, J. E. (1994). Spanking in the home and children's subsequent aggression toward kindergarten peers. *Developmental Psychopathology, 6,* 445–461.

Straus, M. A. (1983). Corporal punishment, child abuse, and wife beating: What do they have in common? In D. Finkelhor, R. J. Gelles, G. T. Hotaling, & M. A. Straus (Eds.), *The dark side of families: Current family violence research* (pp. 213–234). Newbury Park, CA: Sage.

Straus, M. A. (1994). *Beating the devil out of them.* San Francisco: Lexington.

Straus, M. A., Sugarman, D. B., & Giles-Sims, J. (1997). Corporal punishment by parents and subsequent anti-social behavior of children. *Archives of Pediatrics and Adolescent Medicine, 155,* 761–767.

Sue, S., & Okazaki, S. (1990). Asian-American educational achievement: A phenomenon in search of an explanation. *American Psychologist, 45,* 913–920.

Swann, W. B. Jr., & Pittman, T. S. (1977). Initiating play activity of young children: The moderating influence of verbal cues on intrinsic motivation. *Child Development, 48,* 1125–1132.

Thomas, A., Chess, S., & Birch, H. G. (1968). *Temperament and behavior disorders in children.* New York: New York University Press.

Thompson, C. E., & Wankel, L. M. (1980). The effects of perceived activity choice upon frequency of exercise behavior. *Journal of Applied Social Psychology, 10,* 436–443.

Tizard, B., Blatchford, P., Burke, J., Farquhar, C., & Plewis, I. (1988). *Young children of school in the inner city.* Hillsdale, NJ: Lawrence Erlbaum Associates.

Trivers, R. (1974). Parent–offspring conflict. *American Zoologist, 14,* 249–264.

Vallerand, R. J., & Reid, G. (1984). On the causal effects of perceived competence on intrinsic motivation: A test of cognitive evaluation theory. *Journal of Sport Psychology, 6,* 94–102.

Walker, L. J., & Taylor, J. H. (1991). Family interactions and the development of moral reasoning. *Child Development, 62,* 264–283.

Wankel, L. M., & Kreisel, P. (1982, April). *An investigation of factors influencing sport enjoyment across sport and age groups.* Paper presented at the North American Society for the Psychology of Sport and Physical Activity conference, College Park, MD.

Weiss, L. A., & Grolnick, W. S. (1991, April). *The roles of parental involvement and support for autonomy in adolescent symptomatology.* Paper presented at the biennial meeting of the Society for Research in Child Development, Seattle, WA.

White, R. (1959). Motivation reconsidered: The concept of competence. *Psychological Review, 66,* 297–333.

White, S. A., & Duda, J. L. (1994). The relationship of gender, level of sport involvement, and participation motivation to task and ego orientation. *International Journal of Sport Psychology, 25,* 4–18.

White, S. A., Duda, J. L., & Keller, M. R. (1998). The relationship between goal orientation and perceived purposes of sport among youth sport participants. *Journal of Sport Behavior, 21,* 474– 483.

Williams, G. C., Rodin, G. C., Ryan, R. M., Grolnick, W. S., & Deci, E. L. (1998). Autonomous regulation and adherence to medical regimens. *Health Psychology, 17,* 269–276.

Wilson, E. O. (1975). *Sociobiology: The new synthesis.* Cambridge, MA: Harvard University Press.

Winch, G., & Grolnick, W. S. (1993). *Ego involvement, self-focus, and social interaction.* Unpublished manuscript, New York University.

Wolff, R. (1997). *Good sports.* Champaign, IL: Sports Publishing.

Wright, R. (1994). *The moral animal.* New York: Random House.

Xu, J., & Corno, L. (1998). Case studies of families doing third grade homework. *Teachers College Record, 100,* 402–436.

Zuckerman, M., Porac, J., Lathin, D., Smith, R., & Deci, E. L. (1978). On the importance of self-determination for intrinsically motivated behavior. *Personality and Social Psychology Bulletin, 4,* 443–446.

Zussman, J. U. (1980). Situational determinants of parental behavior: Effects of competing cognitive activity. *Child Development, 51,* 792–800.

Author Index

Subject Index